T0131609

WATCHING GOD WOO THE WORLD

An Adult Exploration of God's Grand Story

May the God of steadfastness and encouragement
grant you to live in harmony with one another,
in accordance with Christ Jesus,
so that together you may with one voice glorify
the God and Father of our Lord Jesus Christ.
—Romans 15:5–6 (NRSV)

RUTH E. CORRELL

WESTBOW
PRESS®
A DIVISION OF THOMAS NELSON
& ZONDERVAN

WestBow Press books may be ordered through booksellers or by contacting:

WestBow Press
A Division of Thomas Nelson & Zondervan
1663 Liberty Drive
Bloomington, IN 47403
www.westbowpress.com
844-714-3454

For further information or to contact the author, visit her website http://www.RuthCorrell.com

Scripture quotations are from the New Revised Standard Version Bible, copyright © 1989 National Council of the Churches of Christ in the United States of America. Used by permission. All rights reserved worldwide.

Front cover photograph by Akron Marathon, reproduced by permission.

This book is based upon research done by the author and reported in "That We May Be One: The Power of Gender in God's Story," Trinity Journal for Theology and Ministry, vol. III, no. 2 (Fall 2009), pp. 120–39.

ISBN: 978-1-6642-5687-3 (sc)
ISBN: 978-1-6642-5686-6 (e)

Library of Congress Control Number: 2022902314

Print information available on the last page.

WestBow Press rev. date: 05/10/2022

To probing pilgrims
who delight
the Great Author
when they stumble upon
their true home
in the Grand Story
they didn't write.

CONTENTS

PART II: BLOOD RELATIONSHIPS: THE TUTOR NOBODY CHOOSES

PART III: SEXUAL UNION: COVENANT,
CONTRACT, AND CONCUPISCENCE

PART V: GOD'S GRAND STORY: CLIMAX AND CULMINATION

ABBREVIATIONS USED

Categories and codes of bonds between the genders:

Blood
FD = Father, Daughter; MS = Mother, Son; BS = Siblings: Brother, Sister

Sexual
HW = Married, husband and wife; NM = Not married

The Rest
PP = Peers in the Plot with no blood or sexual connections

Movement from one category to another
PP/HW = Peers in the Plot who then married each other

Lower-case abbreviations indicate the general category,
but with a modification indicated in the story; for example,
a grandparent, an in-law, a half-sibling, a step-relative, or an adoptive parent.

Name/Name = a.k.a., also known as; for example,
Jacob/Israel; Tabitha/Dorcas; Simon/Peter/Cephas

[----] = known only from extrabiblical sources

INTRODUCTION:
BROWSING THE GOOD BOOK

Three True Stories

First: At the laundromat, a man picked up a conversation with me and a friendship began. After several invitations, he let me know he would *not* go to church. One night, he suddenly poured out several agonies he had faced. Without saying so, he believed God had it out for him. His soul simmered with anger and hurt. All I managed to say was, "God *does* love you, and Jesus proved it on the cross." He said nothing.

That spring, he mentioned in passing that he had purchased his nephew's Christmas gift, a Bible story book. I noted he had plenty of time to look it over. Months later, he wrote me that a new colleague at work had invited him to go to church with his family. He had accepted and thought I would like to know. You bet I did!

Second: I was browsing at Hofmann's Catholic Book Store in Erie, Pennsylvania, when a customer approached me with a question. "Do you know if there are any Bible story books here for adults? I heard the Bible has some good stories in it, but it's too much to read the whole thing. All the story books are written for children." Our search turned up nothing for her so I looked on my shelves at home.

I treasure an autographed copy of Eugenia Price's *Beloved World* (Zondervan, 1961) that helped this teenager understand that Christianity is about love, not a list of rules to keep. It's long out of print. In 1995, Walter Wangerin, Jr. published *The Book of God: The Bible as a Novel.* Weighing in at three pounds and 850 pages, it's delightful but daunting. *The Story* published by Zondervan came out in 2001. This substantive abridged selection of biblical readings helps people place events and characters they know in chronological order. Yet its four to five hundred pages still intimidate many readers.

My story: When I was five, my parents gave me a zippered, red-letter edition of the King James Version of the Bible complete with concordance and maps. My name was engraved on the cover. I started by reading the words in red print (attributed to Jesus) in the Gospels and then the stories surrounding those words. The Psalms right in the center of the Bible attracted me, too. The easy-to-read verses go straight to the heart of David and introduce the God who woos the world. These prayers and stories furnish lamps, sofa, wall hangings, carpet, and window dressings for my inner being. In seventy-plus years, they haven't worn out.

The curiosity shown by the woman browsing at Hofmann's and the young man's purchase kept haunting me. They knew the Bible was special, even sacred, but hardly knew where to start. They were not ready to purchase supplementary books about the Bible's historical and cultural backgrounds. In 2004 I started a special research project that might interest these two people and others. The project yielded a list of all the relationships between men and women in the Bible that made a small to great difference. The list grew to over four hundred examples. Most are found in this book, and they will be connected with each other and embedded in the whole of the biblical account. Similar situations may still plague and inspire us today.

Thoughtful adults consider what ideas and beliefs will direct their lives.

- Is there a Supreme Being? If so, what is the character of this Being?
- How worthy of my trust and confidence is the God of the Bible?

- Why would one believe God watches over, listens to, and guides people?
- What differences would it make if I have faith that God loves me?
- Does Jesus Christ still heal body, mind, and spirit today?

These are ultimate questions. The answers we formulate affect our sense of worth and well-being, the decisions we make, and the way we live. The Bible records characters who asked one or more of these questions and what happened as a result.

Ultimate issues may lie behind a desire to read the Bible, but the Bible is neither written in a Q&A format nor organized into "how to" categories. Plus, it was written centuries ago in cultures different from our own. Yet the human race has not changed beyond recognition in the past four thousand years.

Selection of Stories

Reference books list all the biblical examples of men, women, children, kings and queens, books and chapters, trades and occupations, holy days and holidays, apostles, doctrines, miracles, prayers, promises, and parables. But these alphabetical lists are not usually embedded coherently in the whole of God's Grand Story.

Authors of every Bible story book select certain stories and omit others. Here are four reasons I selected accounts that feature both men and women. Almost daily we are bombarded with reports here and around the world of harmful encounters between the sexes: bullying, abuse of power, trafficking, neglect, homicide and suicide, family breakdown, exploitation, rape, pornography, and domestic violence. These problems cause further difficulties with success in school, mental and physical health, family solidarity, loneliness and isolation, the economy, poverty, and legislation at local, state, and national levels. Though the Bible includes X-rated stories and sensuous descriptions of sexual encounters, it never appears in the pornography section of magazine racks. Why? The Bible was not written to hook purchasers, but to tell the truth about God, men, and women. Its characters don't pose before a camera many times before publication. The biblical goal is wholesome interaction, not sexual exploitation.

Second, the prime, universal, and equally distributed human difference is that of gender. Every human being has a mother and a father—somewhere. In the early years of life, children take in and sort an amazing amount of knowledge from the five senses. When a child links dominance with one set of physical characteristics but not another set, the child will believe some sorts of people are meant to be in charge while others that look different are not. Herein lies a chasm between God's intention for men and women and what typically occurs, and the mischief spreads far and wide.

Third, orthodox Christian theology, among the world religions, *uniquely* posits a Triune Godhead of Father, Holy Spirit, and Son or Word of God, each presented in one of the first three verses of the Bible, respectively. Meditation upon the Holy Trinity calls us to mirror the image of God by living together in loving and dynamic unity. The Bible presents a stark contrast to the sacred literature of other world religions in which women are rarely or never mentioned. This deserves the attention of all students of religion.

Fourth, the selected stories here have at least one male and one female character because that pattern marks the whole of the Bible, beginning, middle, and end. In the beginning, the sequence of creation leads first to man and secondly to woman, Adam and then Eve. In the middle, the heritage of faith leads first to a woman and secondly to a man, Mary and then Joseph. In the end, the union of love leads to the marriage feast of the Lamb, Christ the Groom to Church the Bride. Throughout many women and men appear in stories. Appendix A lists many biblical accounts of men and women that parallel each other in some way.

A Few Words about Stories and the Bible

Classic stories have a beginning, a middle, and an ending. Curiosity keeps the reader turning pages to find out how the problem the story presents in the beginning will be resolved in the end. In the middle, the tensions and complications of the plot rise to a climactic turning point. Thereafter the denouement ties up loose ends, unveils critical connections in the plot, and wraps up the story. Authors hope the story ends to the satisfaction of the readers.

The Bible is the magisterial prototype. Though told by many authors over hundreds of years in many genres, the overarching story does have a definite beginning, middle, and end.

In Genesis, God the Father creates the universe, life, and humanity by divine directives.

In Matthew and Luke, God the Spirit conceives the Incarnation outside human causation.

In Revelation, God the Son conquers evil and death with incorruptible love and life.

God's Grand Story begins with the primordial excellence of creation and ends in the mystical glory of the new creation. The problem is human alienation from God that surfaces in myriad ways. The middle is God's unfolding plan to solve the human problem. It culminates when God intervenes by coming as a human being to live here with us at a particular time in human history. The tension of conflict between God and humanity rises dramatically over the thirty-plus years Jesus of Nazareth lived from his birth to his death. The climax is a grisly crucifixion that culminates when the tomb bursts wide open with Resurrection. The denouement continues to unfold around the world, and even Jesus did not know how many centuries would pass until the end, or, more accurately, until the new world under God unfolds completely.

Biblical subplots teach us by example what human alienation and reconciliation with God look like. Modern stories focus on the change in one or two characters. By contrast, when God enters the story, frequently every character in the story may be affected. Beware!

How to Use This Book

This guide book features seventy-plus selected Bible stories. Six in each chapter reflect a common characteristic. Most chapters then annotate six related "Supplemental Stories." Part I's chapters alert you to characteristic themes in God's work in history with individuals and groups. Parts II–IV examine significant connections between the genders in chronological order of their prominence. Part II looks at family relationships: fathers and daughters (FD), mothers and sons (MS), and brothers and sisters (BS). Part III weighs sexual encounters: husbands and wives in marriage (HW) and liaisons not in marriage (NM). Part IV observes other connections between genders of peers in the biblical plot (PP) in the Old Testament,

Gospels, and remainder of the New Testament. Part V surveys accounts of restoring life commonly attributed to God's power and the Resurrection. The Conclusion reviews seminal points the biblical stories illustrate. I recommend reading the first three chapters in their entirety. Thereafter pick stories that interest you. Keep this book as a companion to your Bible for future stories to read.

This book contains minimal instructions and commentary, much like my parents when they handed this five-year-old the zippered black Bible with my name engraved in gold letters on the cover. However, they did expose me to teachers, preachers, Sunday School, summer youth camp, and church services. If you are not currently a part of a faith community, check out web sites of nearby churches. Clergy will be pleased to respond to a call from anyone with a question about the Bible. You may make their day. Your questions may also be answered by resources readily available on line. Discussing these stories with someone else or a small group makes for thoughtful conversations. Yet I can't resist giving a few pointers for interpreting biblical narratives.

• • •

Tips for Interpreting and Reflecting on These Stories

1. The story happens first; the theology comes afterward. The Israelite slaves walked away from their masters without bloodshed. Jesus lived, died, and rose. What these two unparalleled events reveal about God and ourselves is never depleted.

2. To understand a story, it is essential to identify its genre; e.g., teaching story, poetry, parable, sermon, song, creed, apocalypse, history, essay, letter, biography, anecdote, figurative and symbolic, etc.

3. The Bible was not written just for professional theologians, but for all people. Scholars can help us tremendously to understand the background and meaning of a narrative. Take into account that they reflect their sponsoring institutions.

4. Biblical stories, remembered for piercing pungency, present imperfect humans as *examples*. Jesus is the only *model*. See 1 Corinthians 10:11.

5. How you interpret a story might reveal more about you than about the story. Be careful to note mentally where the text stops and your imagination begins. Take time in silence to reflect on how a story may be reading you and working on you.

6. Never base a major belief or doctrine on one story alone. This book models reading several examples before drawing any conclusions.

7. Every Bible story can be seen from three perspectives bottom to top: the characters in the immediate situation; the community that recorded this event for future generations; and the overarching purpose in God's Grand Story to bring all people home to God's realm. Each perspective expands understanding.

8. **God is the hero of every correctly interpreted Bible story.**[1]

The following C's offer various methods to reflect upon these timeless stories. Try them out two or three at a time to see if they help you.

Collect: Gather your Bible and writing tools. Invite God's presence.

Connect: Read the story's introduction and the biblical account straight through.

Concentrate: Examine a character of each gender in a slower reading.

- Imagine this person's thoughts, feelings, desires, and resistances.
- What direct or indirect attention did each person pay TO God?
- What direct or indirect attention was given BY God in this event?
- Which of the four songs in chapter 1 would your chosen characters sing?

Clarify: Observe the whole story's direction and purpose.

- In one word, identify the primary problem; e.g., scarcity, doubt, fear, injustice.
- Trace the arc of the plot: the conflict, climax, denouement, and conclusion.
- How satisfactorily is the problem resolved? What factors are left unresolved?
- How does the story move *into* or *away from* the arc of God's Grand Story?

Confer: Ponder the Puzzler, with someone else if possible.

Check: Review your conclusions for consistency with the text.

Contemplate: Assess the story for its ring of truth and overall merit.

Commend: What lesson(s) in the story recommend preserving it?

Compare: How does the story contrast or connect with others in the chapter?

Close: Note date(s); record memory jogs, reflections, and questions about the story.

• • •

Final Notes about Bible Versions

Many translations and paraphrases of the Bible are available today. Versions vary in spelling of proper nouns. This book uses spellings and wording from the New Revised Standard Version unless otherwise stated. This translation bears official recognition in both the Roman Catholic Church and many Protestant churches. However, Roman Catholics recognize the books in the Apocrypha, but this book does not include apocryphal stories. References here are given in book, chapter, and verse(s) format; e.g., 2 Samuel 6:12–23 (Second Samuel chapter 6, verses 12 through 23); Matthew 5–7 (Matthew chapters 5 through 7); 1 Corinthians 10:1–9, and 13 (First Corinthians chapter 10, verses 1 to 9, and chapter 13); and John 14:1—16:15 (long dash indicates the reading extends past chapter breaks according to usage in the 1979 *Book of Common Prayer*). A few paraphrases do not mark chapters and verses.

Bible versions take into consideration levels of reading skill. Before purchasing a Bible, ask about its grade level. Read a few chapters of the Gospels in a translation for clarity in expression and size of print. Also check out ease of turning pages and a binding that allows the book to lie open at any page. You may prefer an electronic version.

Extra materials like a concordance (a list of key words that identifies the references in which the key word is used), maps, and study helps are often well worth spending more on a Bible. Ready, set, GO!

Author's Note

Prepare yourself for culture shock. Most of us grow up where God is largely absent in conversation (except as an expletive) at the dinner table or restaurant, in the bedroom, marketplace, classroom, media, workplace, health facility, court room, and even the church. By contrast, in the Bible, God lives, breathes, creates, heals, chronicles, communicates, intervenes, and acts upon matter (like wind and rain, land and sea, plants and animals, flesh and mind).

Upon opening the Bible, you enter a world with a joltingly different approach to our lives. In our day-to-day cause-and-effect domain, we meet family and friends, eat, wash, learn, read, work, play, love, hate, choose, ignore, ponder, admire, appreciate, enjoy, exercise, travel, communicate, and finally die. Each of us is the main character in our story that explores our heritage, aptitudes, and vocations. It recounts our choices about how we live, what we do, and what we leave behind. That's our story, beginning to end. Or is it? Could there be more? Yes, I believe there is abundantly more. In Bible stories, one can hardly escape the notion that all its characters participate in a narrative much larger and greater than their own stories.

This is God's Grand Story which began before human history and continues today. God is both the author and the main character. Therefore, the final outcome of individuals, families, cities, and nations ultimately rests in divine hands. Never fear, you can rest assured that the Author desires only your good. Remember John 3:16 (King James Version): "For God so loved the world, that he gave his only begotten Son, that whosoever believeth in him should not perish, but have everlasting life." But that skips too far ahead. For now, let's just say this. In this book, God's Grand Story refers to the long-running, star-studded, drama of God's epic efforts to woo the human race, person by person, nation by conflicted nation. The Bible, written over two millennia by many people, gives witness to the character, actions, and purposes of this God. However, the biblical narrative, from the depths of its horrors to the heights of its grandeurs, confirms Shakespeare's observation, "The course of true love never did run smooth."

Exploring parts of the Bible, whether as a doubtful observer or hopeful participant, offers more than we expect. No tricks or passwords or magical prayers are necessary. It only requires what all narrators ask of their audiences—willing suspension of disbelief. Even though these stories come from a counter intuitive world, the characters and situations can resonate deeply today. Consider that a personal invitation to enter God's Grand Story.

Take time often to pause and ponder as you read. I don't want to hurry you or twist your arm to believe. Not when the Almighty Hero chose suffering and rejection over coercion. The greatest story ever told emerges larger than life and lasts longer than time. Enter it at risk of being surprised by faith, love, and hope.

PART I

GOD'S GRAND STORY: TRANSCENDENCE, TRANSITION, TRANSFIGURATION

The world we live in is at odds with the purposes of the God revealed in the Bible. As a result, the work of the Holy Trinity is to bring about change in individuals and groups *from* being at odds with *to* being in harmony with this loving God. In chapter 1, God's *transcendence* enables access to the physical bodies of characters. These joy-producing events set landmarks in the whole of God's Grand Story. Chapter 2 portrays characters facing *transitions* that change their circumstances and view of God. Chapter 3 chronicles remarkable *transfiguration* of heart, mind, and action. Any of these three movers and shakers addressed in this part of the book may cross your path or have already have changed your life.

Transcendence does not have to be dramatic, but it does capture our attention. Our five senses usually have a role. The risen Lord was recognized when Mary Magdalene *heard* his voice; the couple from Emmaus *saw* his scarred hands break bread; Thomas *touched* his wounds; and the disciples *smelled* and *tasted* fish Jesus ordered. Manifestations of God's presence may break through in the scent of a delicate flower, images from a telescope or microscope, touching expressions of love, or inspired creativity. Ask Handel where *Messiah* came from.

Transition does not have to be traumatic, but it does move us along. Abraham packed up the family; run away Hagar returned; Hannah offered her son to God; Ruth made a commitment; Mordecai repented; Pentecost turned the world upside down. Transitions may be welcomed or dreaded, and they *will* happen anyway. Our movements might be geographic or socio-economic or psychological or political or relational or in outlook or focus or any combination of these. In hindsight we can often identify pivotal points that changed the course of our lives.

Transfiguration does not have to be fantastic, but it does alter us distinctly. When Jacob awoke from the dream of a ladder of angels at Bethel, he hallowed his stone pillow with oil, and his slow metamorphosis began. Joseph recognized his brothers, but they did not recognize him or their own reformation until he tested them severely. Jacob's family story ends in peace and hope only because Esau forgave Jacob, and Joseph was reconciled with his brothers. Though often silent and nearly imperceptible, transformation cannot occur without our minds, wills, and hearts granting consent. A flash of insight, a heightening of senses, a sharpening of reality, or an inbreaking of truth compels us to note this landmark along our paths.

I recommend that you explore these three chapters sequentially. They give the gist of the major events and intentions of the Bible. Thereafter, browse and sample stories as you like. Chapter 12 is essential to God's Grand Story so please take a good look there.

1

Transcendence: Markers and Joy Makers

Fasten your seatbelts as we whiz through the biblical story marking four singular turning points, one at the beginning, two in the middle, and one at the end. In each case, God made use of a person's body to craft a similar but categorically different human being. Each time, the new being elicited an ecstatic exclamation from the viewer. In this chapter, we will look at six such exclamations, which I call songs. The songs give voice to transcendent joy.

"Transcendence" comes from the Latin prefix *trans* meaning "beyond" and *scandare* meaning "to climb" so one witnesses something that goes toward or comes from a source surpassing human origination and expectation. While transcendent experiences can be awesome, they may understandably raise a stumbling block to willing suspension of disbelief. They may set aside the norms of the physical universe on purpose to capture our attention. During transcendent manifestations, people may report the loss of their sense of self and the passage of time while they are enveloped by communion with an intangible sovereignty greater than themselves.

Bernard of Clairvaux (1090–1153), a spiritual master of the twelfth century, examined human relationships with God and found that a person may move in halting movements of two steps forward one step backward through four degrees of love.

First degree—love of self for self's sake (self-centered love);
Second degree—love of God for self's sake (dependence on God's goodness);
Third degree—love of God for God's sake (awe of God's holiness); and
Fourth degree—love of self for God's sake (bonded in God's love).

The four new categories of human beings in this chapter illustrate this progression.

The exact words of the six exclamations called songs are italicized for emphasis in the quotations at the beginning of each featured story in this chapter. Now look at the first human words recorded in God's Grand Story, a song of delight, excitement, and pleasure.

Note: Review the tips on the dog-eared pages, xvi–xvii.

Adam's Song: First Degree of Love—Love of Self for Self's Sake

Then the man said, *"This at last is bone of <u>my</u> bones and flesh of <u>my</u> flesh;*
This one shall be called Woman, for out of Man this one was taken."
—Genesis 2:23; emphasis mine based upon Hebrew syntax stressing possession[1]

The Bible begins with three connected foundational stories whose interpretations fill innumerable pages and hours of teaching. Recognized as sacred in all three monotheistic religions, this is the most famous and widely incorporated narrative in the world. You could sit and soak in these three chapters for the whole of your life and keep discovering insights.

Genesis 1:1—2:3 takes a cosmically transcendent perspective. It introduces the protagonist called "God," Creator of the cosmos. Creation culminates with the blessing of human beings created in God's image. They are called to be fruitful and to care for earth and its creatures. The story ends with God setting apart the seventh day for rest and contemplation.

Genesis 2:4–24 climbs down from the beyond to shape a human being from the earth. Its immanent perspective indicates direct person-to-person presence at the moment. Here we are introduced to the *covert* antagonists called "the man" and "the woman." The divine name used here is "Lord God," a word too sacred to be uttered by a faithful Jew. This story institutes marriage and sets boundaries for sexual intimacy between men and women.

Genesis 2:25—3:24 drops even lower as the archenemy, called "the serpent," slithers out from under the earth to tempt the naked woman and laid bare man. This temptation to doubt the goodness of God's intentions leads to their *overt* disobedience to the Lord God.

These accounts introduce the archetypal protagonist, antagonists, and archenemy. This story of mythic proportions truthfully portrays the root problem of human desire for autonomy and the futility of attempts to cover up that willfulness before each other and God. Then God provides an immediate remedy by tailoring a covering for them from torn flesh over spilt blood, an act that foreshadows the ultimate solution to come by the seed of woman. The healing process between God and humanity fills the rest of the Bible.

This simple but profound account grasps both the attention of preschoolers and the fascination of philosophers. To credit its origin merely to genius falls short of the mark.

Puzzler: From one human being comes two like but categorically different human beings, man and woman, each with an inner urge to merge with the other. The story asserts that such unity requires boundaries. Why? What evidence can you find to ascertain whether Adam's song *about* God and Eve, but not *to* either of them, issues from love or lust?

Mary's Song: Second Degree of Love—Love of God for Self's Sake

And Mary said, *"My soul magnifies the Lord, and my spirit rejoices in God my Savior,*
for he has looked with favor on the lowliness of his servant.
Surely, from now on all generations will call me blessed;
for the Mighty One has done great things for me, and holy is his name."
—From Mary's well-known *Magnificat* in Luke 1:46–55, verses 46–49

No woman in history has inspired more works of art portraying her face, posture, and devotion than the favored one whom God destined to be the mother of Jesus. She prophesied accurately that henceforth "all generations will call me blessed." The birth narratives are found in Luke 1:5—2:52 (Mary's story) and Matthew 1:1—2:23 (Joseph's story).

Between Genesis 1–3 and the opening of the New Testament, many centuries passed. Luke 1 places Mary within the larger story of a worshiping community with long-standing traditions and leadership. Scribes had carefully recorded examples of how their Good Shepherd's guidance, protection, discipline, and instruction had preserved their nation. Drawing upon this heritage prepared Mary's heart and mind to believe Gabriel's astounding message.

In her precarious situation, God anticipated her need for more affirmation, so Gabriel gently pointed her to a devout elderly relative, Elizabeth, who was also having a miracle pregnancy. The moment Mary crossed her threshold and called out a greeting, transcendence enveloped them. Even before hearing Mary's whole story, Elizabeth and her unborn son confirmed Gabriel's message. Then Mary burst into her glorious song with joyful confidence. Her song does not focus on her child to be born without the benefit of sperm. It expresses radical faith in the promise of a holy God to her ancestors.

Such is the way of the Good Shepherd, who kept past promises and looked ahead to arrange for Mary's future. The favor of the Most High overshadowed this supreme woman, smoothing the road to marriage with Joseph, supplying gifts from wise men far away for provision, protecting them from King Herod's hostility, and giving her a home with the apostle John after the sword pierced her soul as Simeon had prophesied.

Puzzler: John's Gospel, written years after the others, reflects on Jesus's virgin birth with new insight. He writes: "... to all who received [Jesus], who believed in his name, he gave power to become children of God, who were born, not of blood or of the will of the flesh or of the will of man, but of God" (1:12–13). Contemplate being born anew with the purity of the Holy Spirit upon you and the power of the Most High overshadowing you (Luke 1:35).

Resurrection Songs: Third Degree of Love— Love of God for God's Sake

The conquest of the powers of evil came to a climax when Jesus snapped the chains of death by rising from the dead after three days in the tomb. As portrayed at the opening of Mel Gibson's *The Passion of the Christ*, Jesus's bruised heel crushed the head of the serpent as the LORD God promised in Genesis 3:15. Only the Holy Trinity could forecast the intervening years between the promise and its fulfillment. This transcendent action plan prepared a particular worshiping community and the watching world for the centerpiece of history, the Resurrection.

His followers recognized him, if not at first, yet also realized that he was now categorically different from his previous self. His body was impervious to death and unbound by the physical world and its limitations. No ghost or hallucination, he talked, explained, instructed, cooked, ate, and met with individuals and groups, sometimes by appointment. These dramatic encounters validated the truth of Gabriel's message to Mary. Her son must be the Son of God. The exclamations in the following three featured stories trace chronologically his followers' growth in comprehending the incomprehensible.

> Mary Magdalene's Song (John 20:1–3, 11–18)
> The Duo's Song (Luke 24:13–35)
> Thomas's Song (John 20:19–29)

The disciples involved recognized Jesus Christ primarily through use of one or more of the five senses. He was physically present to them. In each encounter he delivered a different message. Before his death he frequently told his disciples and those he healed *not* to say anything about what he had said or done. But now each event was immediately shared with other disciples.

Mary Magdalene's Song

Jesus said to her, "Mary!"
She turned and said to him in Hebrew, *"Rabbouni!"* (which means Teacher). ...
Mary Magdalene went and announced to the disciples, *"I have seen the Lord ..."*
—From John 20:1–18, verses 16, 18a

This brief drama has given me jubilant chills since childhood. When no one else was at home, I acted out this first encounter with the risen Lord many times. The stone fireplace in the living room is the open tomb. Coming down the steps from my bedroom, I apprehensively approach the spooky stones. Imagine the background music. Tears blur my eyes; I cannot even do for Jesus the last service of preparing his body for burial. Then I hear the "gardener" speak from the dining room. I plead indignantly, "My Lord is gone. Where have you laid him?" The music stops. "Mary!" The response goes beyond my acting ability to put into body language the fear, the anger, the joy, the astonishment—and the hurt when he tells me not to hold on to him. No! He's going away again? Isn't everything going to be like it used to be? But he is *alive*! I run out the back door and announce the news to the disciples hiding in the garage.

Bad news, good news, bad news, denial, and the need for company. It's typical of the roller coaster after a death. Mary must have been mentally, physically, and emotionally drained to the last drop. In her grief and anger, she could not see how dangerous it would be to harbor Jesus's dead body. The religious and government authorities had sealed up the tomb just so the disciples could not steal his body and then proclaim that he had risen. The risk involved was insane! Jesus had once cast out seven demons from her. Had the aftermath of a traumatic death and the shock of a fleeting meeting with Jesus opened the door for those seven to return?

At times like this we feel helpless, but Jesus knew what to do. He commissioned her with a message to deliver. As she ran, she repeated Jesus's reassuring words. "I am ascending to *my* Father and *your* Father, to *my* God and *your* God" (emphasis mine). Later the disciples understood that Jesus's death and Resurrection did make them blood-related but not by hemoglobin: "Love is that liquor sweet and most divine, / Which my God feels as blood; but I, as wine."[2]

Puzzler: Traditions stabilize expectations and offer something to hold on during the emotional turmoil of bereavement. Ignore them at your own risk. But the comfort of sticking to "the way things are done" can block apprehending a greater good. Speculation about Mary Magdalene often consumes more energy than this event. What human tendencies make conjecture about her sex life more appealing than this monumental encounter?

The Duo's Song

They said to each other, *"Were not our hearts burning within us*
while he was talking to us on the road,
while he was opening the scriptures to us?"
—From Luke 24:13–35, verse 32, Cleopas and unnamed companion, probably his wife

One purposeful meeting at a time. After seeing Mary Magdalene, Jesus met alone that morning with Simon Peter, who had denied him three times.[3] What transpired is none of our business. The disciples would be under surveillance the moment news of the missing body reached officials. They dreaded what a living Jesus would think of them for they had failed to pray for him and then had abandoned him. What a babble of charged emotions all of this elicited!

Jesus knew that only his forgiveness, if they could believe it, could bring peace to their guilt-ridden hearts. It would help them to understand that his innocent death and Resurrection comprised the climax in the plot of God's Grand Story. While this truth could put the events of the past three days in perspective, none of them were in state of mind for a prolonged lecture on the concept of Messiah in the Hebrew Scriptures. Jesus waited for the right time and situation.

So his next move was to fall into step with a couple returning from Jerusalem to their home near Emmaus. Little did they know that this meeting was anticipated before the foundation of the world. Each step added geographical and emotional distance between themselves and the ferment. Each footfall on dusty *terra firma* brought them closer to daily reality. The two of them were ready to talk and think things through. A hike of at least two hours provided enough time for a refreshing look at God's Grand Story. All things considered, certainly it was best for their concentration that they were kept from the shock of realizing who was walking with them.

Jesus encouraged them to express their disappointment and dashed hopes. His gracious listening earned him the right to chide them, "Oh, how foolish you are, and how slow of heart to believe all the prophets have declared!" Really? Instantly their minds snapped to attention. Was there more to the story? They insisted that he stay with them. At dinner, they noticed the scarred hands breaking the bread and knew who had been opening the Scriptures to them!

Puzzler: Jewish law required two witnesses to test the validity of a testimony. Jesus disappeared when these two caught on so they had enough time to return to Jerusalem. The Synoptic Gospels (Matthew, Mark, and Luke) record a similar sequence of events in the life of Christ. It takes just 1½ hours to read Mark, 2 for John, and 2½ for Matthew and Luke (because each adds material of his own). How might there be a direct link between this couple and the Gospels?

Thomas's Song

Then [Jesus] said to Thomas, "Put your finger here and see my hands.
Reach out your hand and put it in my side. Do not doubt but believe."
Thomas answered him, *"My Lord and my God!"*
—From John 20:19–29, verses 27–28

Thomas was a believer. He believed in Jesus from early on, after Jesus's first miracle of turning water to wine at a wedding. But after the very next event John records, he indicates that the disciples' belief fell short of solid consistency. John says it was only after the Resurrection that they *really* believed.[4] Believers believe, at least sometimes. But when God upsets the equilibrium, we wonder about believing. Thomas is us!

Several characteristics of Thomas make me like him. First, he did not believe everything he heard. Fake news began in Genesis 2, and Thomas applied wise misgiving. Second, nevertheless, he maintained contact with the disciples to hear all they could tell him about that matchless first day of the week. Third, he resisted wishful thinking, a.k.a. denial, which is typical during grief and crisis. In the aftermath of Jesus's death, this man, known to have a pessimistic streak,[5] had gone the gamut of emotions from misery and despair to hopes too good to be true. For a week, he thought of little else. Fourth, he knew himself and trusted his close friends enough to admit freely that he needed extraordinary help to believe. That may have been easier for a twin growing up with discerning, blunt feedback from his double. Fifth, he made a boldly unambiguous statement of what he needed. The matter was far too important for him to accept secondhand testimony. Jesus, who knew he was telling the truth, accommodated him! Jesus also made sure the rest of us Thomases found that out. Finally, Thomas earns my respect and admiration because he immediately responded wholeheartedly to Jesus Christ. This thoughtful pessimist was first to recognize the risen Christ for who he was, his Lord and God.

Thomas must never have tired of telling others the blessing Jesus gave to all those who believe without putting their hands in his side. The church he founded in India has survived uninterrupted to this day. Thomas's story presents the pinnacle of the purpose of John's Gospel. The remainder of the book, however stirring, is a personal postscript.

Puzzler: "Unless I see the mark of the nails in his hands, and put my finger in the mark of the nails and my hand in his side, I will not believe." We aren't given any clues for the tone of voice Thomas used: defiance, arrogance, weariness, depression, resignation, self-doubt, or despair. Try these out to see the difference it makes. So why weren't we given any such stage directions?

The Saints' Song: Fourth Degree of Love— Love of Self for God's Sake

From the throne came a voice saying,
"Praise our God, all you his servants, and all who fear him, small and great."
Then I heard what seemed to be the voice of a great multitude,
like the sound of many waters and like the sound of mighty thunderpeals, crying out,
"Hallelujah! For the Lord our God the Almighty reigns.
Let us rejoice and exult and give him the glory,
for the marriage of the Lamb has come, and his bride has made herself ready;
to her it has been granted to be clothed with fine linen, bright and pure"—
for the fine linen is the righteous deeds of the saints.
—From Revelation 19:1–10, verses 5–8

Toward the end of the apocalyptic visions recorded in the Revelation, we hear the voices of newly made immortal human beings. These last human words addressed to God exalt the Almighty. At last good has conquered evil, and the choir anticipates the consummation of love when saints and their Redeemer will be united forever. The course of true love endures. These choristers remained faithful and obedient to the end despite plagues, persecution, martyrdom, and tribulations too many to list. Spanning history, they hark from every nation and tongue. Their names are recorded in the Book of Life. The apostle Paul wrote, "When this perishable body puts on imperishability, and this mortal body puts on immortality, then the saying that is written will be fulfilled: 'Death has been swallowed up in victory.' 'Where, O death, is your victory? Where, O death, is your sting?'"[6] The Saints' Song surpasses all others in ecstatic joy.

The words *my* and *me* disappear in praises to the Lord, *our* God. United in one voice immortals lose themselves in transcendence far greater than themselves. Finally, as intended from the very beginning, men and women together bearing the image of God serve as ministers who reign with Christ. From his exile on the island of Patmos, St. John the Divine leaves us with a message. Take courage, the Alpha and Omega will make good on every promise.

Puzzler: We can no more comprehend such glories than an unborn baby can imagine ice cream sundaes, sunsets, and first kisses. Like that baby's, our equipment to conceive the home Christ is preparing remains not fully developed. For now, we must make do with images we know: fruit, trees, dragons, swords, fire, cups, thrones, feasts, weddings, and garments that make us look our best. Go ahead, fearlessly imagine the ways death conquered imitates yet transcends birth.

2

Transition: Crises and Pivotal Points

While there is disagreement about the degree of historicity of the early chapters of Genesis, it is hard to disagree with the truth of the problem in the seminal stories of the Garden of Eden, the Flood, and the Tower of Babel. To their own detriment, humans persist in wanting to arrogate God. To address the problem, God set apart a family whose reason for being was to bless the world by living under the terms of a covenant with God. God promised to preserve the descendants of Abraham and Sarah, and they promised to obey. They followed the covenant much of the time and ignored it at other times. Obedience brought blessing and sustaining power even when they faced difficulties and hostility. But when they strayed from the Good Shepherd, devastating circumstances eventually caught up with them.

The stories in the Hebrew Scriptures (Old Testament) come from the perspective of Abraham and Sarah and their descendants. The Bible chronicles this family as it grew to be a clan, tribe, nation, and finally a dispersed group that still maintains its identity in Judaism. God kept the covenant faithfully through seven distinct eras. Five Old Testament eras of disrupting moves made them more dependent upon God. The two New Testament eras put into effect a superior covenant toward which God had been moving all along.

First era: Founders

Abram/Abraham's family leaves everything behind to go to a new land.

Second era: Exodus

Moses leads the family's descendants out of slavery in Egypt.

Third era: Judges

Judges defend and rule the twelve tribes that spread throughout Canaan.

Fourth era: Kingdom

Kings rise to reunite the tribes into a nation governed from Jerusalem.

Fifth era: Exile

The two divided nations are defeated and sent into oblivion and exile.

Sixth era: Incarnation

Jesus is born in Judea into the regathered remnant now under Roman rule.

Seventh era: Church

The early church under persecution flees throughout the Mediterranean.

Disruptions can be reality checks in which a person moves toward or away from faith. This chapter features men and women in the crisis of transition whose obedience proved God's trustworthiness. Their critical decisions preserved the community of faith at pivotal points.

From this point forward, the types of connection between male and female characters are listed at the beginning of each story and labeled with a two-letter abbreviation for each of the six possible general categories. For easy reference, the back cover of this book lists them.

First Era, Founders: Abram/Abraham and Sarai/Sarah

HW, Abram & Sarai / Abraham & Sarah	NM, Abram & Hagar	PP, Abimelech & Sarah
HW, Pharaoh & Sarai	MS, Hagar & Ishmael	MS, Sarah & Isaac
HW, Lot & wife	ms, Sarah & Ishmael	PP, Isaac & Hagar

Story: Spans Genesis 11:26—23:20. Note particularly 11:26—13:4, 15:1—18:15, 20:1—21:21, 22:1—23:20, 25:7–11. Added insights: Isaiah 51:1–2 and Hebrews 11:8–12.

Setting: Nomadic clans headed by family patriarchs lived in tents while seeking pasture for their herds. Disputes with other clans arose about use of land and wells. The rugged habitat hid predators, so hospitality was a life-and-death matter for travelers. Everyone stayed prepared to offer accommodations. Hoping to appease the gods, fertility cults offered sacrifices of animals, even children, with prayers for wealth from fertility. Worship of riches has a long shelf life.

In the first half of the second millennium BCE, God called Abram to leave his home city and go to a land God would show him. God promised that his descendants would bless the whole world. Later his wife Sarai, his nephew Lot with his family, and their servants accompanied Abram into Canaan. Abram built altars for worship and prayed to the LORD, but Sarai remained barren. He amassed great wealth in livestock and a band of servants to protect them. Then God changed the founders' names to Abraham and Sarah with assurance that she alone was co-recipient of the covenant with their *many* descendants. But ten years passed with no baby.

Today Abraham is revered as founding father of the three monotheistic world religions of Judaism, Christianity, and Islam. But I wouldn't want to be married to him. Husbands owned wives, but a good cow was worth more than a gorgeous, but barren, wife. Twice he attempted to pass her off onto nearby suzerains. Both reprimanded him when his premeditated exploitation caused problems. God upheld marriage bonds even without offspring, but what of the promise?

Since it seemed God wasn't coming through, Sarah gave her husband to her Egyptian maid, Hagar, in her stead. Hagar bore Ishmael. But then at last Sarah, in old age, gave birth to a miracle son, Isaac. Tension between Hagar and Sarah and between Ishmael and Isaac came to a final breaking point. On Mt. Moriah, Abraham's faith was severely stretched, but he trusted that Isaac would receive the covenant as God had promised.

Puzzler: Imagine that Isaac comes back home and reports to Sarah that on Mt. Moriah God provided a sacrifice to spare his life. She had risked her life to bear Isaac with little hope of surviving childbirth. What might she want to say to Abraham now? Fast forward. The only land he ever owned, he purchased to ennoble her burial. He refused to accept it as a gift or to bargain down the price (and he could bargain!). How had dynamics between them changed over time?

Second Era, Exodus: The Two Families of Moses

PP, Pharaoh & Shiphrah, Puah	MS, Moses & Jochebed	PP, Moses & 7 sisters
PP, Baby boys & midwives	BS, Moses & Miriam	FD, Jethro & Zipporah
HW, Amram & Jochebed[1]	ms, princess & Moses	HW, Moses & Zipporah
	FD, Pharaoh & princess	

Story: Spans Exodus–Deuteronomy. Read Exodus 1–4, skim through the events of the Plagues, Passover, and Red Sea crossing, and pick up again at chapters 16–20.

Setting: Ancient Egypt's highly developed civilization produced wonders of the world, and its pyramids were meant to last forever. The Nile River provided water, transportation for wide-flung commerce, and fertile land by its regular flooding. Egypt's polytheistic religion held that a dying person crossed the Nile to the afterlife. Division of labor placed shepherds at the bottom of the social heap and priests with magicians near the top under the Pharaoh.

After Abraham and Sarah, three generations followed, headed by the patriarchs Isaac, Jacob, and his twelve sons who took the name God gave to their father, Israel. These families' stories are rife with conflict stemming from marital problems, favoritism, envy, deceit, greed, revenge, and ambition. Finally, a severe famine forced Jacob's family to move to Egypt, a captivating account of God's provision despite the family messes. Because they were shepherds, they had to live apart from the Egyptians in Goshen, the Nile's delta.[2] Separation sustained their identity through language and stories of their early ancestors passed down orally.

Eventually their numbers increased to a threatening level, so Pharaoh enslaved them. His fear continued, so he decreed that all Hebrew baby boys be thrown into the Nile. Fearless midwives and one family resisted infanticide. In contrast to the founders' families, this family displayed mutual support and dauntless faith. To cut a long story short, Pharaoh's daughter adopted the baby and paid his mother to nurse him. Educated by his slave mother and by Egypt's palace, Moses grew up bi-cultural. Thus, God specially prepared him to confront Pharaoh and to lead the Israelites out of slavery. Passover celebrations endure to recount this great deliverance. Since then, no society's moral code has surpassed Moses's Ten Commandments.

Puzzler: Read Hebrews 11:23–29. People outside the Israelites also served God. Jethro, a.k.a Reuel, the priest of Midian, extended hospitality to the conflicted and desperate fugitive, Moses. Neither slave nor king, this sonless father of seven daughters offered his wisdom before, during, and after Moses's momentous decision to obey God's call. What short- and long-term purposes may God have had in providing Moses with this particular father-in-law?

Third Era, Judges: Honor to Degradation

After Moses died, his longtime assistant, Joshua, became the leader of the twelve tribes of Israelites. He helped them to begin occupying Canaan when they finally arrived after two generations of wandering in the wilderness. At his first and most famous battle, the people marched around the walls of Jericho as God commanded, "and the walls came a'tumblin' down." Before Joshua died, each of eleven tribes had been allotted a territory to occupy near the Jordan River. Distributed among the territories, the priests, descendants of Levi, were to lead worship according to the covenant with God. Local judges rose up to settle disputes and to lead them in battles against their enemies. It was a good plan on papyrus, but the dispersed Israelite tribes lacked the discernment and resolve to resist the abhorrent practices of nearby tribes.

During the last third of the second millennium BCE, Canaanite tribes boasted of their fertility gods and orgiastic worship. Their idols spotlighted the tribe's wealth in resources and skills in workmanship. However, the tables of the Ten Commandments enshrined in the Ark of the Covenant forbade worship of any manmade images and required sole worship of the one LORD God who had delivered them from Pharaoh by powerful signs and wonders. Although news of their escape from Egypt spread and generated some respect, the stories eventually lost currency as generations came and went. An invisible God with no power or wealth to spotlight opened the Israelites to self-doubt and scorn from other tribes. Furthermore, the Ark often rested miles away. In peacetime, living near idol worshipers led to intermarriage. In wartime, casualties left women behind as loot to take as extra wives and concubines. God's people seemed not to realize fully that they were walking an extremely perilous path to disunity, total assimilation, and disappearance of their covenantal identity. As they forgot the LORD, everyone, even the priests, did what was right in their own eyes.

The ancient Jews deserve admiration for their honesty and humility in preserving cautionary tales of pathetic Jephthah, strong but stupid Samson, and worse. To counterbalance these examples of infidelity in this era, biblical treasures include touching accounts of Hannah and Ruth. The impact of their faith set stagnant streams in motion to form a river of living water, and Israel's wasteland became a verdant pasture. Their stories have inspired countless souls in distress to harbor hope in the gracious God who never reneges on the covenant.

The book of Judges graphically demonstrates the deterioration of dealings between the genders. Appendix D traces the slippery slope from honor to degradation. It can be optional reading because of its X-rating for sexual content and violence. Chapter 4 lists three supplemental stories for those who prefer not to plow through the entire book of Judges.

From Judges to Kings: Hannah and Samuel

HW, Elkanah & Hannah	PP, Eli & Hannah
HW, Elkanah & Peninnah	MS, Hannah & Samuel

Story: Spans 1 Samuel 1:1—25:1. For crucial moments, read chapters 1–3, 7–12, and 15–16.

Setting: The Philistines living along the Mediterranean coast sought additional land to the east. They had developed the most advanced metallurgy and weaponry among the various groups in Canaan. Their aggression threatened Israel's judges and the kings to come.

A woman was dependent first on her father, second on her husband, and finally on her sons, another well-intentioned plan that looked good on papyrus. But during the perilous era of Judges, many fathers, husbands, and sons died in war, leaving behind destitute women. Hannah's husband, Elkanah, loved and favored her, but she was barren. His other wife, Peninnah, produced several children, and she rubbed this in to torment Hannah. When the family went to Shiloh for annual worship, Hannah entered the temple to beg God for a son. When she departed, she had promised to give up the hoped-for son to God's service for his *entire life*. She had laid aside the plan on papyrus and had cast her fears about the future upon God. In an amazing turnaround, she returned to her husband in good cheer. Try that some time.

Every year when she delivered a new coat to Samuel at the temple, Hannah could remind him of God's answer to her prayer. Throughout his life, he repeatedly prayed, "Speak, for your servant is listening." He traveled among the tribes teaching God's ways and bringing reform. The people had confidence that Samuel truly heard and spoke God's word. A crisis came when the tribes demanded that Samuel give them a king like other tribes. "No," Samuel argued. "The LORD is our sole ruler, and kings will require much to support their palaces and armies." They refused to listen. Since they had rejected the LORD as king, God told Samuel, "Listen to their voice and set a king over them."

When King Saul disobeyed God, Samuel grieved. Once again, the aged man laid aside his preferences to anoint the young shepherd, David, as the second king. Samuel's prayerful courage and humility guided Israel's transition from a tribal to a national structure. His crucial leadership followed his mother's example in laying aside her agenda to trust God.

Puzzler: Hannah's prayer in the temple is the only instance in the Bible of a silent prayer. Perhaps she had no means for the required offering accompanying a vow. From what you know of prayer (or emergency rooms), what can make a praying person look and act drunk? This happened again when the Holy Spirit came upon the disciples at Pentecost.[3] What indicators of experiencing the visitation of God's Spirit appear in Hannah's situation?

Fourth Era, Kings: Ruth to David

HW, Elimelech & Naomi	HW, Chilion & Orpha	ms, Naomi & Boaz
MS, Naomi & 2 sons	PP, Boaz's foremen & Ruth	PP, near-kinsman & Naomi, Ruth
HW, Mahlon & Ruth	PP/HW, Boaz & Ruth	MS, Ruth, Naomi & Obed

Story: Book of Ruth. Later chapters will feature Boaz and Ruth (p. 62), Ruth's ancestry through Lot (p. 35), and Boaz's ancestry through Rahab (p. 79).

Setting: In the era of the kings, 1050–586 BCE, tribes became kingdoms like Israel, and kingdoms became empires, like Assyria and Babylon in Mesopotamia. Aggression from these powerful empires continually encouraged various alliances among the smaller nations. Roads, such as the King's Highway and its crossroads, increased commerce. Income from tributes and tolls vacillated depending upon which king gained control of the trade routes. King Saul united the Israelite tribes, and King David defeated the Philistines to the west. Israel's location on this heavily travelled crossroads of the north, east, and south by land and west by sea brought prosperity. Israel traded its barley, wheat, olives, dates, grapes, and pomegranates for cedar from Lebanon, spices from the east, and luxurious ivory from Africa.

Saul became increasingly unstable and envious as David, the singing shepherd and harpist, gained popularity. After Saul and his son died in battle, the power struggle for the throne came to a head, but David was not of royal blood. Furthermore, bad blood from Ruth, his Moabite great-grandmother, flowed in his veins. David and his family had also taken shelter in Moab. This story defended and established the legitimacy of David's lineage. Now rewind to the era of Judges. Three sonless widows related by marriage must choose where to live, and their two native lands follow different gods and laws. Two laws in Israel fuel the plot. First, reapers had to leave behind the corners of fields and grain that fell so the poor could glean food. Ruth gleaned. Second, the Levirate marriage law called for a "kinsman redeemer" to purchase the land of a man who died without children and/or to marry his widow. The kinsman's son by the widow owned the land in the name of the deceased. Boaz, a kinsman, admired Ruth for trusting "the God of Israel, under whose wings you have come for refuge!"

King David's Psalms echo his great-grandfather's words.[4] David's dynasty led to Solomon's Golden Age and to Jesus. In God's Grand Story, belief trumps blood and birth order.

Puzzler: In Ruth, the mirrored decisions of two daughters-in-law and two kinsmen-redeemers illustrate crossroad choices. The heritages of Hannah's radical trust in God's provision and Samuel's patient listening bear fruit in Ruth and David. What qualities do you suppose God recognizes in those who venture out of their comfort zones by faith?

Fifth Era, Exile: Ahasuerus, Mordecai, and Esther

HW, Ahasuerus & Vashti	PP, Shaashgaz & Esther	PP, Haman & Esther
PP, 7 attendants & Vashti	HW, Ahasuerus & Esther	HW, Haman & Zeresh
PP, 7 lawyers & Vashti	PP, Bigthan, Teresh & Esther	PP, Harbona & Esther
fd, Mordecai & Esther	PP, Esther's eunuchs & maids	PP, Haman's 10 sons & Esther
PP, Hegai & Esther	PP, Hathach & Esther	

Story: Book of Esther.

Setting: After King Solomon's reign, the kingdom split into the northern Israel and the southern Judah. In 722 BCE, Assyria defeated Israel and deported the nobility. In Judah, a series of forced exiles to Babylon led to its fall in 586. In 539, Babylon fell to Persia. Kings Cyrus and Darius permitted exiled people to return to their homelands. Some Jews stayed put, but about 50,000 soon returned to Jerusalem. Despite local opposition, they worked to rebuild the city walls and temple under the able leadership of Ezra and Nehemiah.

It is likely that Ahasuerus was King Xerxes, son of Darius, who ruled the huge Persian Empire in 486–465 BCE. The suspenseful story begins with a lavish feast that may have been a war council to plan a massive attack on Greece in 483. Xerxes's wife gave birth to Artaxerxes in 484–483, one explanation of Vashti's refusal to appear. Furthermore, Persians, heavy wine-bibbers, customarily reviewed war plans under the influence. War began well by burning Athens. But after defeat at Salamis, Persia retreated in 479. Esther became queen upon the return of a defeated, debt-laden king. Xerxes's volatile temper is well documented. Beware!

An urban Jewish official in Persia wrote Esther sometime after 460 BCE, when Ezra returned to Jerusalem, and before 311, when Persia fell to Greece. Ambitious Mordecai, named after the Persian god Marduk, kept his religion quiet until he needed a reason for defying Haman, a descendant of Israel's ancient archenemies. He changed Hadassah's name to Esther, after the Persian "star" or the Babylonia goddess Ishtar. Ironically, secular Jews in high places in the winter palace of Xerxes at Susa saved the struggling pious Jews back in Jerusalem. God remains hidden but unmistakably at work overturning unalterable laws of Persia and turning a pogrom, the worst threat Jews had ever faced, into a holiday of feasts and gift-giving, ebullient Purim.

Puzzler: A traitor to Greece helped Xerxes win at Thermopylae, but he was assassinated by his chamber guards. In a culture of intrigue, greed, and power politics, how does a king govern and keep his skin intact, especially after defeat and huge losses to the state treasury? Examine the story for examples of self-preservation and control versus courage and vulnerability. How does trust, or lack thereof, change every main character and the Persians in this amazing story?

Sixth and Seventh Eras: Life of Jesus and the Early Church

The bridge between the Old and New Testaments spanned about 400 years. During that period, no major or minor prophet arose to proclaim oracles from God. After Persia fell, the repatriated Jews struggled to maintain their religion and practices under Hellenistic rule. When their temple was desecrated, the Jews revolted in 166 BCE under the leadership of the priestly Maccabees. Eventually Israel, now called Judea, was given autonomy and independence. By 40 CE, Rome had taken the regions bordering the Mediterranean Sea and ruled in Judea. Even though Rome required recognition of Caesar as a "Son of God," they tolerated Judaism. Jews could practice and worship according to their own laws, but only the Roman ruler could order an execution. People paid both Roman taxes collected by despised tax collectors and a Temple tax. An uneasy balance of power persisted between Rome and the ruling Jewish body, the Sanhedrin.

The Sanhedrin had basically two parties. The aristocratic Sadducees concerned themselves with political and economic matters but did not believe in supernatural beings and life after death. The Pharisees concentrated on interpreting the Law and teaching devotion to Jewish practices which embellished the Law with rules that affected daily life in every respect. Herod the Great began construction of the Temple in Jerusalem in 20 BCE. The magnificent structure was completed 46 years later. Its presence dominated and centralized Judaism and offered an incentive for Jewish acquiescence to Roman rule.

Into this setting of resented Roman rule and an increasingly compromised and legalistic Judaism came the birth of Jesus. When Herod the Great learned from the wise men and the Temple scribes that a new king of the Jews might have been born in Bethlehem, he executed all its male children younger than two years old. But Joseph, warned in a dream, had already fled to Egypt with Mary and Jesus. Herod's son and grandson were equally brutal rulers. Less than 50 years after completing the Temple, the Romans burned it down in 70 CE because of Jewish insurrection. With the self-imposed massacre of loyalists at Masada around 73, the Judaism Jesus knew ended.

Nevertheless, while the Prince of Peace walked this earth and for decades beyond, the minimal military expansion during the *Pax Romana* made possible the golden age of Rome. The "Roman Peace" from 27 BCE to 180 CE provided Greek as a unifying language, widespread law and order under Roman rule, more roads and shipping routes throughout the Empire, aqueducts to deliver water to growing cities, and prevalent exchanges of ideas and learning. "But when the fullness of time had come, God sent his Son,"[5] in no small part because of these favorable historical conditions. The good news of the Resurrection of Jesus Christ spread faster and wider from city to city than it could have in any previous time in history.

So now it is time to read a Gospel. Here's my suggestion. Begin by asking the Holy Spirit to guide you. In making your choice, start by looking over the beginning and ending of each Gospel, especially the way Jesus is introduced and the conclusion.

Matthew 1:1 and 28:16–20: *From* Jesus, the Messiah, son of David, son of Abraham, *to* the Great Commission to teach and baptize everywhere in the name of the Trinity.

Mark 1:1–11 and chapter 16 (shorter ending): *From* Jesus Christ, Son of God, *to* proclaiming everywhere the good news of eternal salvation.

Luke 1:1–4 and 24:44–49: *From* an orderly account of fulfillment *to* witnessing to all by understanding the Scriptures in the power from on high from the Holy Spirit.

John 1:1–14 and 20:30–31, 21:24–25: *From* the Word became flesh *to* belief that this record is truthful in its offer of eternal life through Jesus.

The first three Gospels (called the Synoptics) follow the same general outline beginning with John the Baptist, then Jesus's Galilean ministry of healing and teaching with parables, the choice of disciples, the Transfiguration, the foretelling of his death, his focus on training the disciples, the journey to Jerusalem, his controversies with religious leaders, and the events of Passion Week leading to his death, burial, the Resurrection, and the Ascension. Except for the birth narratives, almost all of Mark is in Matthew and Luke. Matthew adds teachings like the famous Sermon on the Mount, and Luke adds beloved parables such as the Good Samaritan and Prodigal Son. John, writing later, assumes his readers know these accounts. He focuses on noteworthy events that served as signs to reveal Jesus's identity and purpose as Messiah, the Savior.

Residence of the Holy Spirit: 120 at Pentecost

PP, the eleven remaining apostles (after Judas's suicide), Joseph/Barsabbas/Justus, and Matthias with other men & Jesus's mother and certain other women = 120

Story: Luke's second volume, The Acts of the Apostles, continues from the Ascension in Luke 24:50–52 into Acts 1:1–11 and on to Pentecost in 1:12—2:47.

Setting: Acts tells the history of the early church. After the Resurrection, Jesus's friends expected that he might appear among them at any moment. They learned to act in ways that welcomed his presence and formed new habits of words and deeds that would linger after Jesus departed from them permanently. He ascended 40 days later, and told them to wait for the coming of the Holy Spirit to empower worldwide witness.

A Jewish synagogue required at least ten men. The 120 early believers could yield one group for each apostle—except women counted! Both men and women were involved in proposing who might take Judas's place. After this decision, they continued praying for ten days until the Feast of Pentecost. This annual festival drew dispersed Jews from around the world. They celebrated the early harvest in the growing season and God's giving of the Law to Moses. Thus, it was the perfect setting for the first harvest of new believers in Jesus Christ, who fulfilled the Law and more.

On the morning of Pentecost, the Holy Spirit empowered all 120 men and women to speak in other languages so that everyone at the Temple could hear about Jesus in their own mother tongue. They gossiped the Gospel among the thousands who were milling around the Temple courtyard. The 120 fulfilled Joel's prophecy of witness from men and women, high and low, young and old. The once cowardly Peter erupted in a courageous sermon offering repentance and forgiveness for killing Jesus. Among the crowd stood those who had seen his attack in the Garden of Gethsemane and had heard his denial of Jesus. He was the prime example of transformation from denying disciple of Jesus of Nazareth to avid apostle of Christ the Lord. The other 119 believers and many others echo him and have taken God's Grand Story to the uttermost parts of the earth.

Puzzler: Many dramas throughout the centuries have portrayed the events of the Gospels and Acts: healings, teachings, the Passion, and Resurrection. Some depict the slow-to-learn disciples becoming eager-to-witness apostles who will die for their faith. I wonder why God did not wait for video recording before sending the Messiah. What was gained by depending upon in-person word of mouth to spread the story of Jesus?

Supplemental Stories

Review the four degrees of love of self and God in chapter 1. The following stories provide more examples of people in crisis whose decisions moved a community forward or backward on God's path. How did these characters' actions and decisions affect the quality of faith that emerged from this pivotal situation?

Noah, Three Sons and Wives (HW, MS, fd)
Era: pre-Abraham. Story: Genesis 5:28—9:28.
What pitfalls did this family avoid that angered God? Why do we forget God's promise for orderly seasons and delight in the promise the rainbow represents?

Pharaoh and Shiphrah, Puah (PP)
Era: Exodus. Story: Exodus 1.
A dangerous social chasm yawns wide when two slave women who served other slave women defy Pharaoh. Does God really reward lying and civil disobedience? Why?

Nabal, David, and Abigail (HW, PP/HW)
Era: Kingdom. Story: 1 Samuel 25:2–42.
King Saul's jealousy forced David and his comrades to live as fugitives. How does the character of each key figure here have an immediate and long-term impact?

Solomon and Foreign Wives (HW)
Era: Kingdom. Story: 1 Kings 10:14—12:19.
Solomon proved Samuel's prediction correct that kings would cost the people their wealth. Now be honest. What parts do wealth and greed play in marriage choices?

Daniel, Belshazzar, and Queen Mother (PP, MS)
Era: Exile. Story: Daniel 5.
In exile, Daniel rose to high positions because of his administrative skills and ability to interpret dreams. How does remembering protect people today?

Paul and Women in Church (PP)
Era: Church. Story: 1 Corinthians 11:1-16; 1 Timothy 2:8—3:15.[6]
In Ephesus, the temple to the Goddess Artemis, with only women priests, dominated religion. Paul balanced the gender scales. Don't miss the endnote on this debated passage!!

3

Transfiguration: Conflict and God's Intentions

God's promise to Adam and Eve and the covenant with Abraham and Sarah's descendants ensured hope for blessings and an identity that would survive all the surrounding peoples. Chapter 2 has traced God's people from one family to a flourishing kingdom, from defeat and exile to a returning remnant in Judah, and from independence under Maccabean rule to Roman domination. Then in the fullness of time God came to earth in Jesus. While Matthew 1:1–17 traces the descendants of Abraham forward to Joseph, Luke 3:23–38 traces the ancestry of Mary back to God.

Jesus's ministry of healing and teaching extended God's mercy to all who put their faith in him regardless of their backgrounds. His redemptive death and Resurrection endowed family status based not upon bloodline but upon trust of *Our* Father in heaven. According to John's Gospel, a new birth by the work of the Holy Spirit bestows power to be a child of God. This new identity may seem to assert itself effortlessly, but the course of true love involves internal conflict.

According to Jesus, a self-centered, self-promoting, and self-protective human being (that would be all of us) must die. "If any want to become my followers, let them deny themselves and take up their cross daily and follow me. For those who want to save their life will lose it, and those who lose their life for my sake will save it. What does it profit them if they gain the whole world, but lose or forfeit themselves?"[1] Fortunately, we are also self-aware and can invite change. This new birth into God's family brings about family resemblances by transfiguring our *invisible* thoughts, desires, dispositions, and motivations. People with transformed hearts make *visible* the image of Christ.

The stories in this chapter portray conflicts that escalated to the point of desperation, deadliness, even murderousness. Eventually, these people faced a choice to release their grip on anger, deceit, greed, bitterness, vengefulness, or desolation. In some cases, they met inescapable consequences of their wrongdoings head-on. In other cases, crushing responsibilities or unjust situations threatened to overwhelm them with hopelessness. God pursued them until they granted permission for divine intervention within them. This process brought both transitory and enduring character transformation but not without their braving change, vulnerability, and humility.

That is how the Triune God woos the world, by loving us into the worldwide family of those who call God our Father. Together Three Persons bring one willing human being into the family. The process is labor-intensive for us, but glorious.

Jacob and Three Generations of Conflict

MS, Rebekah & Esau, Jacob	HW, Jacob & Leah, Rachel	FD, Jacob & Dinah

Era: Founders, including four generations: Abraham and Sarah; Isaac and Rebekah; Jacob and Leah, Rachel; 12 sons and Dinah, other daughters

Story: Jacob appears in Genesis 25:19 and dominates chapters 27–35, especially 28 and 32–33. Chapters below will feature other connections in Jacob's family: Rebekah and Esau, Jacob (p. 43); Jacob's sons and Dinah (p. 51); and Jacob and Leah, Rachel (p. 23).

Setting: In nomadic life, a child logically would marry within the clan for common language and traditions. Thus boundaries of incest were much looser then than now. A fertile marriage provided laborers during life and heirs after death, the more males the better to care for the livestock. Animal husbandry required arduous 24/7 attention.

Of all the family, Abraham's grandson, Jacob, stirred up the most conflict. He was the younger of twins and envied the double inheritance allotted to the firstborn, Esau. To achieve his desires, he cheated, lied, and manipulated—skills learned at his mother Rebekah's knee. She hurried him off to her brother's home to escape Esau's anger. Laban outmatched Jacob in trickery. After working seven years to marry his daughter, Rachel, Jacob woke up to a surprise the morning after the nuptials. Rivalry between his two wives and their surrogates kept traffic heavy in Jacob's tent. The result was twelve sons and several daughters. A pattern of suspicious watchfulness simmered between the father-in-law and son-in-law until Jacob fled with his family. When his sons despicably betrayed a neighboring clan over a perceived insult to Dinah, their revenge made Jacob's name odious enough that once again, he was forced to leave.

All these troubles might be attributed to his mother, his wives, and his daughter, but Jacob knew better than that. When Jacob had nowhere to run but back toward home, he learned that Esau was coming to meet him with 400 men. At the end of his rope of deceit, pride, and cleverness, Jacob wrestled all night face to face with God and begged for a blessing. God was not about to bless Jacob's character. God changed his name from Jacob, "supplanter," to Israel, "wrestles with God." The name Israel lives on today. We know of no more lies from Jacob, but he suffered grief from family problems for years to come.

Puzzler: Though we can grudgingly admire Jacob's cleverness, we can barely avoid smirking when he gets his just deserts. But the wrestling match is different. It is a solemn, even terrifying matter to approach the Holy One, and one is never the same again. Reread Genesis 33, counting the number of times Jacob called himself Esau's servant or called Esau his lord. How did God's action both transfigure and protect Jacob's life?

The First Four Sons of Leah

FD, Laban & Leah, Rachel	HW, Jacob & Leah	HW, Jacob & Rachel
nm, Jacob & Bilhah	nm, Jacob & Zilpah	FD, Jacob & Dinah by Leah
The women who bore Jacob's 12 sons listed in birth order:		
#1–4 MS, Leah & Reuben, Simeon, Levi, Judah	#5–6 ms, Bilhah & Dan, Naphtali for Rachel	#7–8 ms, Zilpah & Gad, Asher for Leah
#9–10 MS, Leah & Issachar, Zebulun	#11–12 MS, Rachel & Joseph, Benjamin	

Era: Founders

Story: Genesis 29–30; 33; 35:16–26, 49:29–33. See also Deuteronomy 21:15–17.

Setting: Fertility bestowed God's blessing, and sons ensured future security for women. Enter mandrakes. This plant has a forked taproot that resembles the lower half of the human body. Superstition valued its odor as an aphrodisiac to stimulate sexual activity and fertility. Its use in magic, witchcraft, and occult practices triggers narcotic and hallucinatory effects and induces soothing sleep. But there has always been more to marriage than what procreation and mandrakes offer. Marital hopes await currents of loving and being loved.

Leah's poignant situation saddens and infuriates me. It was bad enough that she had no choice about her husband. In those times, at least the groom *wanted* the bride, but Leah was deliberately denied that, too. Jacob had worked for seven years to marry Rachel, but Laban deceitfully used Leah to wring seven more years of free sweat out of Jacob. Daily Leah watched Jacob's eyes turn to her sister. Since divorce was forbidden to women, she had no escape. Her transformation occurred over several heartbroken years, but the story is told in a mere five verses (29:31–35). Observe the painful progression of names she gave to her first four sons. She believed that God heard her cries and cared for rejected women like Hagar.

Slowly the locus of her focus shifted from her husband to the *true* source of unconditional love, the LORD. At last, she realized that *only* God could meet her heart's desire. Lifting praise to the LORD, she etched a laudable name into the soul of Judah. As we are prone to do, Leah and Rachel slipped back into their rivalries. In the end, the LORD esteemed Leah's devotion. Full of years, Jacob would lie in his grave with Leah, not Rachel. Through Judah's line, Leah is immortalized as a direct ancestor of King David and Jesus Christ.

Puzzler: People who have been rejected by essential people in their lives struggle to believe that God unfailingly extends love to them. How can they recognize what they have never experienced? Rejection feels like unworthiness, if not condemnation. How is it that Leah neither fell into believing she deserved her lot nor resorted to giving up on God—or even Jacob?

Judging Judah and Tamer Tamar

HW, Judah & Shua's daughter	HW, Er, Onan & Tamar	fd/NM, Judah & Tamar
MS, Judah's wife & Er, Onan, Shelah	bs, Shelah & Tamar	MS, Tamar & Perez, Zerah

Era: Founders

Story: Genesis 38. The story is tucked into that of Joseph in chapters 37–49. Contrasting Judah's actions in 37:12–36 with those in chapters 43–44 reveals his astonishing character change.

Setting: This region is vulnerable to drought, but Egypt normally had the advantage of the flooding Nile River. Even in a prescientific world, people studied cause and effect. The priestly class observed carefully and gained status as they made use of predictions, dream interpretations, and magical arts. Joseph's skills confounded the Egyptian priests and lifted him to second only to Pharaoh. In the story of Tamar, like Ruth, Levirate marriage was sometimes ignored for a widow from outside the tribe. But God had far better intentions in mind.

You did *not* learn about Tamar in your tender Sunday School years, but you certainly learned the story of Joseph and his coat of many colors. The trouble started when Jacob's heart-throb, Rachel, finally had a son. Jacob made Joseph a princely favored child and gave him a special robe. Its long sleeves indicated that he did not have to do rough outdoor work. Little wonder he had grandiose dreams that infuriated his older half-brothers. Judah, with his brothers, instigated a plot that would get rid of Joseph plus give them a tidy sum of silver without actually killing him. Like father, like son—to Jacob's inconsolable grief.

Tamar entered several years later. Faced with his trail of illicit actions, Judah humbly confessed to Tamar's town, "She is righteous, I am not."[2] To say this of a woman he considered an inferior outsider and worse was transfiguring. In the end, the threat of starvation forced Joseph's older brothers into a dreaded confession to their father. Tamar's bold action was the catalyst to transformation and a joyous mending of Jacob's fractured family.

The course of true love can run over rocky roads. Judah needed a total makeover, but his heavenly Father was up to the task. Someday God's Grand Story will bring everyone to their knees. Meanwhile, when you hear Judah's name, praise the LORD. Leah will smile!

Puzzler: You now have read most of what Genesis tells us about the founders of Israel. Along their nomadic paths, they built altars for burnt sacrifices to give gratitude and devotion to God. Their invisible God had given neither the Ten Commandments nor codified worship. Yet the LORD kept forming and reforming them. When in your life have you seen transformation as radical as Judah's? How believable is his story?

King Josiah and Prophet Huldah

PP, Manasseh & mediums	fd, Shallum & Huldah
PP, Manasseh & goddess Asherah	PP, men & women singers
PP, Josiah (with his highest officials: Hilkiah, Shaphan, Asaiah, Ahikam) & Huldah	

Era: Kingdom

Story: 2 Chronicles 33–35 (also found in 2 Kings 21–23).

Setting: King Solomon's son Rehoboam placed a heavy tax burden on the people, so the northern tribes rebelled in 930 BCE. Jeroboam initiated a new dynasty and set up worship in Bethel, a site sacred to Jacob/ Israel. The southern tribe of Judah maintained David's dynasty from Jerusalem. Both kingdoms fell into idolatry and the orgiastic cults of neighboring nations. I will leave it to your imagination to interpret the symbolism of ritual poles in the groves at the high places. In 722, Assyria defeated Israel, dispersed the nobility, and relocated other people there. After Josiah's reign (640–609), Babylon destroyed the temple and exiled the Judeans by stages under puppet kings. By 586, only the poor were left in Judah, and many fled to Egypt.

No king before or after Josiah "turned to the LORD with all his heart, with all his soul, and with all his might, according to all the law of Moses."[3] Upon hearing the book of the Law, he tore his clothes, an act of contrition and humility reminiscent of Adam and Eve's awareness of their nakedness. He ordered repair of the Temple, demolition of the high places, destruction of the idols, incineration of religious articles, and deposition of the mediums, wizards, priests of Baal (male) and Asherah (female), and the host of heaven. In deference to the high respect accorded to prophets, he dispatched his highest officers to Huldah to hear from the LORD. She lived in the quarter of priestly Levites, and her family had responsibility for vestments. The devoted Huldah encouraged Josiah with God's promise of peace in his lifetime. After the nation recommitted to the covenant, they kept the most magnificent Passover since Samuel's time.

Josiah's worthy last-ditch efforts ended at his death 13 years later in 609 BCE. The laments of men and women singers enshrined his legacy. Nevertheless, reform from the top down is hard to maintain, and the history of ingrained sin eventually brought disaster.

Puzzler: Thus far, the stories have chronicled God's transforming work with individuals. In this story, hearing the Law of God focused King Josiah's goals. With penitence, he devoted his reign to reformation of the places of worship and a national remembrance of God's deliverance at Passover. In your life, what places, objects, and rituals have opened a window into the unseen spiritual world, for good or ill? What particular ones would you willingly abolish?

The Wedding Steward and Mary

(HW, groom & bride)	PP, steward & Mary	MS, Mary & Jesus
PP, disciples & Mary	PP, men & women servants	

Era: Incarnation

Story: John 2:1–12.

Setting: After all these serious stories ending with death, we need a joy break. Jews both mourned and celebrated with vigor. Weddings epitomized joy at the high point in one's life. Servants labored long to prepare food and wine enough for seven days of partying. If the wedding steward ran short, he would be the object of jests forever. When all was ready, the groom fetched the bride from her home. The whole village entered the wedding procession through the streets to his family's home. The local rabbi even halted lessons so the boys could join in. Virgins usually married on Wednesday. In the middle of their first week of marriage, the rabbi gave newlyweds special blessings on their first sabbath. While close friends stayed all seven days, other guests received a welcome and blessing whenever they arrived.

Mary's family were among the guests at Cana along with Jesus's disciples. Hosts liked to invite a rabbi with his disciples. Even though the servants had been watering down the wine, it ran out. The women's quarters were located near the stored wine, so Mary noticed the steward in a sweat. Had the servants been secretly sipping the supply? Guests were expected to help with provisions so she headed to Jesus. The Son of God politely but firmly declined. Nobody wants to have to go to work during a party! Seriously, the first miracle he performed publicly would also be his first step toward the cross. Only the disciples and servants (who get good press in the Bible) ever knew what actually happened. I picture Jesus giving the exonerated servants an innocent shrug of his shoulders with a surreptitious wink. The family escaped curious questioning by departing. Rather than heading south to Nazareth, they headed north along the international transportation artery to Capernaum for a few days at the seaside.

John writes the word "love" more than any other biblical author. How like him to make a groom and bride the locus of the focus for Jesus's first sign of his mission. Jesus came to woo the world his Father loves so much. And what a wedding there is yet to be!

Puzzler: See point 7 on the dog-eared page (p. xvi). Consider how this event enriches the three perspectives from ground to cosmic levels. Stone was the best material for jugs used to keep water for ritual purification, but putting wine in them temporarily defiled them. Here, a vessel of water to purify is transformed to a vessel of wine to gladden the heart, a situation-saving upgrade. What do you make of Jesus dealing out this reversal?

Jesus and the Woman at Sychar

PP, Jesus & woman	PP, disciples & woman	PP, men & women of Sychar

Era: Incarnation

Story: John 4:1–42.

Setting: When Israel collapsed in 722 BCE, Assyria ordered conquered people to relocate. This led to intermarriage that diluted religious heritages in Samaria and elsewhere. The Jews despised these half-breed Samaritans. They followed part of the Hebrew Scriptures and traditions (like Levirate marriages) but worshiped in their own temple on Mt. Gerizim. Sychar lay at its foot. Ongoing conflict between the Jews and Samaritans had damaged their respective temples. In Jesus's time, Samaritans held land sandwiched between Judea to the south and Galilee to the north. Jews went out of their way to avoid contact with them. God had other intentions.

Like the previous story, this one features a common item, a water jug. It was the conversation starter of Jesus's longest dialogue with an individual on record. The seven exchanges between them underscore just the salient points of the extended conversation. The story begins and ends with an invitation. The high point is at the middle exchange, a characteristic of Hebrew storytelling. The woman was amazed when this Jewish male broke a double taboo by talking to her, a Samaritan woman. Her amazement turned to wonder when Jesus revealed that he knew all about her. Her story detailed a larger share of grief, conflict, and rejection than most others. Second marriages happened on Thursdays. She had undergone four such marriages. When a man and woman set up house with resources for neither dowry papers nor a wedding, they were still considered married by the community. Rather than condemning her, Jesus showed that God was seeking people like her who desired to worship in spirit and truth. His offer of living water dispelled her doubts about God's disposition toward her.

To her alone Jesus directly revealed himself: "I am [Messiah], the one who is speaking to you." Anyone else has to come to that realization another way. In awe she sped back to Sychar to tell her neighbors, and the presence of Jesus transfigured the hearts of many villagers.

I wonder if Jesus sent young John back to the well to retrieve the water jug she left behind. What other eyewitness could recall this detail many decades later?

Puzzler: Josiah and Huldah understood that physical symbols and rituals convey spiritual substance. Their efforts corrected the external places and forms for worship. Much later, Jesus repeatedly pointed deeper into the essence of true worship. Silence and solitude may point out the truth about real thirsts. When God's Spirit pays a visit to offer living water, how ready might you be to leave behind your own jug of self-help?

Supplemental Stories

See if you can recall the order of the four degrees of love of self and God. (See Chapter 1 or p. 31 ahead). The stories below involve individuals or groups consenting to or resisting change in attitudes and actions. *Trans*formation here connotes change inspired and empowered by God's intentions for the human race. Resisting change of this type leads to *de*formation.

Moses and Cushite Wife vs. Aaron and Miriam (HW, BS)
Era: Exodus. Story: Numbers 12.
When Moses took a wife from outside Israel, big sister and brother rebelled against their little brother. God's drastic lesson definitively established Moses's preeminence.

Boaz and Naomi (PP/ms)
Era: Judges. Story: Ruth.
In the center of the story (Ruth 2:20), Naomi glimpses hope in Boaz's kindness to Ruth and follows up immediately with proper protocols. Her bitterness changes to blessing.

The Prophet Jeremiah's Sermon (PP, HW)
Era: Exile. Story: Jeremiah 44.
Powerful and prosperous Egypt often attracted the discouraged. After Judah's exile, stern Jeremiah reminded the people who fled south why they had abandoned God's promises.

Father and Mother of the Man Born Blind (HW)
Era: Incarnation. Story: John 9.
Fear of powerful religious authorities kept these parents from rejoicing after their son's healing. Jesus affirmed this rejected man who clung to worship in spirit and truth.

The Jerusalem Council (PP)
Era: Church. Story: Acts 15.
Gentiles' offerings to idols and sexual promiscuity appalled the Jews. The half-brother of Jesus resolved this conflict so the estranged groups could eat and worship together.

Dionysius and Damaris (PP)
Era: Church. Story: Acts 17:16–34.
Paul showed respect for the religious curiosity of these sophisticated Greeks and then introduced the Gospel. Two noteworthy people in this challenging group responded first.

The Summary Commission

Love wins! These three chapters draw the arc of God's Grand Story of wooing the world. Father, Son, and Holy Spirit begin the ball. Leaping and swaying and clapping and pirouetting, the Three move with perfect synchrony in the One divine dance. Each move issues from divine love that wills passionately to remove human and satanic barriers to life and to dress mortals in immortality. Then with a tap on a shoulder comes the invitation to enter the dance. Patiently and firmly, Father, Son, and Holy Spirit teach the steps of the dance that unfolds through the braided trio of transcendence, transition, and transfiguration.

And the dance rises to a rhapsody of joy. Props from Genesis appear renewed in Revelation. Light from God's throne dispels the need for the sun. The crystal-clear River of Life has doused the flaming swords that shut out Adam and Eve. Saints toss off garments of blood-stained animal skins and let the Hero tuck their arms into flowing, glowing gowns of pure white linen. Together they have danced from the first to fourth degrees of loving self and God.

The words *transfiguration* and *transformation* come from the same Greek word and are often used interchangeably. As you continue reading this book, remember that *transformation* is not a buzz word for trivial changes. In this book, *transformation* refers to Spirit-led character changes that occur over time in becoming more like Christ. *Transfiguration* calls up two concrete images. A figure is visible in one way or another as in a countenance of sheer joy or a vision energizing a creative endeavor. *Figure*, as in figuring out something, refers to insights as eyes light up with the solution to a problem and an ah-ha moment of discovery or revelation.

Transcendence, transition, and transfiguration serve up the staples of brief biblical narratives, but over time they yield transformation. The concrete language and imagery of Hebrew narration suit examples well. Therefore, the traveler from Genesis to Revelation can expect short stories of divine encounters (transcendence), major intended and unintended movements (transition), and pivotal changes in appearance or understanding (transfiguration or, alas, disfiguration). Transformation is often described in poetry and prophetic oracles. Also, God's Grand Story is less likely to focus on one character's transformation than on tracing the transformation or deformation of a family, community, or nation. God's intentions keep the rhythms and movements of the covenant with humanity.

Now return to chapter 1 and to the exclamations that punctuate the beginning, middle, and end of God's Grand Story. Review the foci of the four joy-making story markers:

God forms a woman from a part of a man.
A virginal woman gives birth to Jesus, Son of Man and Son of God.
The risen Jesus Christ is recognized by others in his incorruptible body.
The Redeemed put on immortality in God's presence with all the saints.

Dog-ear or mark the next page that traces the four degrees of love in the pilgrimage into the love of self and the Triune God.

Please accept this invitation uttered in unison by the whole company of heaven. This is your commissioning.

The Spirit and the bride say, "Come."
—Revelation 22:17a

In the remainder of this book, you may read the featured stories in any order that interests you. They will be waiting for a curious reader to return to the book after it has been temporarily put aside. As in all timeless and formational literary accounts, transfiguring discovery of meaning and understanding await you year after year. That's a promise.

Therefore, in the blank space after a Puzzler or in the margin of a Supplemental Stories page, write the date(s) you meditated upon this narrative. This record prompts you to trace new and deeper ways a story has affected you over time.

<u>Adam's Song: First Degree of Love—Love of Self for Self's Sake</u>

This at last is bone of <u>my</u> bones and flesh of <u>my</u> flesh;
This one shall be called Woman, for out of Man this one was taken.

<u>Mary's Song: Second Degree of Love—Love of God for Self's Sake</u>

My soul magnifies the Lord, and my spirit rejoices in God my Savior,
for he has looked with favor on the lowliness of his servant.
Surely, from now on all generations will call me blessed;
for the Mighty One has done great things for me, and holy is his name.

<u>Resurrection Songs: Third Degree of Love—Love of God for God's Sake</u>

Mary Magdalene's Song: *"Rabbouni!" ... "I have seen the Lord."*

The Duo's Song: *Were not our hearts burning within us*
while he was talking to us on the road,
while he was opening the scriptures to us?

Thomas's Song: *"My Lord and my God!"*

<u>The Saints' Song: Fourth Degree of Love—Love of Self for God's Sake</u>

Hallelujah! For the Lord our God the Almighty reigns.
Let us rejoice and exult and give him the glory,
for the marriage of the Lamb has come, and his bride has made herself ready;
to her it has been granted to be clothed with fine linen, bright and pure.

PART II

BLOOD RELATIONSHIPS:
THE TUTOR NOBODY CHOOSES

Have you ever wondered why you landed in the midst of people you call mother, father, brother or sister, and son or daughter? We are thrust into close quarters with those who did not choose us and about whom we had no choice. In these blood relationships, we receive and pass on hereditary characteristics. Family members are scarily like ourselves and curiously unlike ourselves. Even the miscarriage and stillborn weigh in as the family story is told or left untold. The power each parent has over a child has varied in cultures over human history. Today ethical dilemmas focus on how much adults can pick the genetics and decide the birth of their children. If you are adopted, your parents knew only a sketchy bit about you when they signed papers to take legal responsibility for your welfare for up to eighteen years and to leave you an inheritance. Is this not an insane arrangement, or is it? What did the Creator have in mind to set life up this way?

The reality is that parents and children are inextricably bound together. There is no such human as a child without a mother and a father figure, no mother without a father figure and a child, and no father without a mother figure and a child. Take away one of the three, and you have none of the three. Does that not mysteriously mirror the eternal bond of the Holy Trinity in whose image we are created? Apparently, the Creator decided humans need to be nested in such relationships. They are worthy of examination.

In a household, we experience and exchange love and hate, honor and anger, justice and jealousy, closeness and alienation, enduring and passing personal histories in the rawest and most transparent manner. Thus, each family member leaves an indelible mark on you and your life story, and you will inevitably leave your own mark(s) on theirs. Underestimating and undermining these foundational relationships incur incalculable damage. How difficult it is to forgive a primary family member who leaves us crestfallen when promises of unconditional love dissolve or are never offered. How can I love myself if I am embittered by those who have formed me? Fears about a Day of Judgment may stem from hurts we have inflicted or failed to forgive among our bone of bone and flesh of flesh. No one can truthfully claim innocence.

The next three chapters explore biblical stories about blood-related people who are not the same gender. Chapter 4 deals with fathers and daughters (code FD); chapter 5 with mothers and sons (MS); and chapter 6 with brothers and sisters (BS). Remember that no family lies outside the reach of God's grace and mercy.

4

Fathers and Daughters: Destination Determiners

The prayer that uniquely identifies Christian worship addresses the One who wishes to be called "Our Father." How real or unreal the God of the Grand Story appears to a person is closely linked to the human being that person calls "father." That is the way words work, and Jesus, the Word, knew this full well. Only Jesus could rightly call God his Father. (The rest of us are offered adoption.) The first and primary lie we believe is that God is like our human father, biological or not, righteous or not. Therefore, blessed be the father who teaches his children directly and emphatically by word and deed that he is NOT God. And blessed be the children of any age who astutely navigate separating their fathers from their Father in heaven, like salt water from fresh water. If you resist this notion, stop now to consider what is true and what is false.

Overseeing the selection of a husband impacted the destiny of a daughter and depended upon the wisdom and resources of her father. Intermarriage with foreigners was frowned upon, not for ethnic reasons but primarily to avoid drawing the coming generation into idol worship. But ethnic solidarity without devotion to the LORD nearly destroyed the tribe of Benjamin in civil war, and the frivolous capture of brides at the end of Judges concluded the foulest story in the vilest era in the Bible. Kings who arranged marriages for political alliances and wealth had few virtuous outcomes in Scripture, if any. Not surprisingly, you will see that marriage partners based on character traits and spiritual formation worked best for the welfare of all. These marriages reflected the inner life of the self-giving Trinity rather than the use of one gender for the advantage of the other and the families involved.

In the following featured and supplemental stories, I recommend at minimum that you compare and contrast the first two fathers. Both fathers and their daughters knew the reality of inexplicable tragedies, but only one family's story *is* a tragedy. The names of both fathers are bywords of informed Jewish and Christian communities. Their wives also gained noteworthy reputations. One advised her husband to "Curse God, and die." Jesus used the other wife as a warning: "Remember Lot's wife." If you don't already know them, here you will learn the back stories that make these quotes endure.[1] Honest self-examination urges us to secure both of them in our quick-access memory file for appropriate application.

Job and Three New Daughters: Trio of Treasures

HW, Job & wife	BS, Job & sisters
FD, Job & first 3 daughters	FD, Job & Jemimah, Keziah, Keren-happuch

Eras: Founders (oral tradition); Kingdom (wisdom literature)

Story: Book of Job. Read the prologue and epilogue in Job 1–2 and 42. Then fast-skim chapters 3–37, slowing down in chapters 27–31. Lean back in a comfortable recliner before the LORD's whirlwind blast of questions in Job 38–41, a lesson in humility you won't forget.

Setting: This timeless discourse addresses a problem just as troubling today as over 3,000 years ago: How can a supposedly just, good, and powerful God who fails to alleviate suffering to our satisfaction be worthy of worship? The inspired author of Job probably used a story passed down by oral tradition and then tapped into the power of poetry to convey the distress that pain inflicts on body and soul.[2] Job's world fits the era of the Founders, while the written style fits the period of flourishing wisdom literature during and after the reign of King Solomon, whose astute judgments gained him wide renown.

The story also raises the inevitable question of God's verdict on those outside the covenant given to Abraham's family. During the animated exchanges between Job and his four friends in chapters 3–37, Job mentions the sacred name, LORD, only once. By contrast, the Israelite author uses the sacred name 25 times in the other chapters. Also, the prophet Ezekiel (14:12–20) warned the Jews in exile that they would not escape the consequences of their disobedience even if the righteous Noah, Daniel, and Job were all living in their midst. Ezekiel drove his point home that *only* those three, primarily *outside* the Abrahamic covenant, would be rescued from disaster. God's favor is not determined along cultural or religious lines.

Indeed, Job received God's favor. This verbosely male story draws to a surprising conclusion. Peeping up through winter's last snow appear three beautiful spring flowers, Job's three daughters. Their names, like Leah's sons, give voice to Job's spirit. Jemimah, "dove," symbolizes peace restored; Keziah, "cinnamon," suggests spice of delight in life, and Keren-happuch, "container of antimony," a big-ticket eyeshadow, invites gazing into the window of the soul. Blessed and esteemed are the daughters of a father who enjoys the LORD's favor.

Puzzler: The book of Job tautly stretches "willing suspension of disbelief." As you assess the end—and beginning—of this account, consider how Jesus might respond. Job blissfully enjoys life with four generations of offspring without ever learning that he defied Satan's predictions. What factors caused the changes between Job's pre- and post-trauma actions?

Lot and Two Daughters: A Caved-in Family

HW, Lot & wife	FD/nm, Lot & 2 daughters
PP, 2 fiancés & 2 daughters	MS, 2 daughters & Moab, Ben-Ammi

Era: Founders

Story: Genesis 13–14, 18–19 (see also Deuteronomy 2:9, 19; Ezekiel 16:46–52; 2 Peter 2:6–11).

Setting: Sodom and Gomorrah were located somewhere in the north-to-south fertile valley of the Jordan River, which flows into the Dead Sea. Running between the Jordan and the Mediterranean Sea, a chain of rugged hills provided grazing land for the livestock of nomads like Abraham. Digging wells exacted hard labor, so water from springs was welcomed and closely guarded. Local groups formed alliances for protection from invaders. Living in tents allowed for continual movement *to* the next grassland or *from* hostile tribes. Not an easy life!

Lot's father died before Abraham and his father left Ur. After Abraham's father died in Haran, Abraham took his nephew into his family, and they traveled southward into the hill country along the Jordan valley. Unlike Job, Lot witnessed his uncle stop to build altars to worship the Lord, and he knew that Abraham embraced the covenant with God. When the feeding needs of their combined livestock caused conflict among their herdsmen, Abraham allowed Lot to choose the land where he would prefer to live. Lot chose the fertile Jordan valley with its cities, commerce, and social life. At first he took his tent there, but before long, he had built a house in Sodom for his wife and two daughters. Eventually, he numbered among the leaders who sat at the city gate conducting trade and handling court cases.

The biblical references above in parentheses give additional insight into both Lot and Sodom. Though Israelites considered Sodom and Gomorrah abhorrent, prophets often assessed the covenant-breaking Israelites as worse than these cities. Even though Lot rose in prominence in Sodom, he remained an outsider tormented in his soul by conditions there. Arrangements for his daughters to marry local men proceeded before the rapid downward spiral that led to disaster. By physical force, Lot's family survived except for one. Job wrestled with God in his pain, but the depleted Lot succumbed to fear and alcohol. God's grace prevailed, protected, and preserved this despairing family. From Lot and his older daughter would come Ruth, David, and Jesus.

Puzzler: Abraham cared for Lot and intervened more than once on his behalf. His earnest prayers for Sodom yielded a promise that Lot's family would be spared. The morning after the disaster he scanned the smoking cities from the hills. He hoped in vain to spot Lot approaching. Instead Lot had hidden away in a cave rather than return to his generous uncle. From beginning to end of this story, what counsels can you glean from factors leading to this tragic situation?

Jethro/Reuel and Zipporah: The Third Family of Moses

PP, Moses & 7 daughters of Jethro	FD, Jethro & his 7 daughters
HW, Moses & Zipporah	MS, Zipporah & Gershom, Eliezer

Era: Exodus

Story: Exodus 2–4, 18.

Setting: The Red Sea forms the border of Egypt on the west and the Saudi Arabian Peninsula on the east. At the northern end of the sea lies a wedge of land where the traditional location of Mt. Sinai is thought to be. Jethro lived in Midian on the far eastern shore of the Red Sea across from the wedge. Water ran underground and in streams coming down the mountain in the rocky desert, providing pastures for grazing animals.

When Moses fled the furor of the Pharaoh, he passed Mt. Sinai and crossed into safety at Midian. The arduous trek gave Moses time to review both his Hebrew and Egyptian heritages. The abject servitude in which his people lived unjustly kindled embers in his soul. Little did he suspect God was showing him this land where he would one day lead the Hebrews into freedom. By a well in Midian he witnessed male injustice against girls. The son of two mothers who had resisted Pharaoh's orders to save his life grabbed his staff instinctively. His Egyptian martial arts drove the scoundrels off in terror. Enter Jethro, the father of the seven girls and the local priest.

Like Job, this priest from outside the Hebrew traditions had taught worship of God to his daughters. With good discipline, he rightly instructed them to search for their rescuer in order to offer him hospitality. The two men discovered a kindred respect for the one true God, and Jethro entrusted his firstborn to Moses. When the embers in Moses's soul burst into flame at the burning bush, Jethro recognized God's call on Moses. He willingly sent Moses, Zipporah, and their two sons to Egypt with his peace. But having only daughters, Jethro had not practiced circumcision. At a spiritual crisis point, Zipporah relieved the tension for Moses by stopping to circumcise their sons. As Pharaoh's hostility heated up, Jethro welcomed Zipporah and her grandsons back for protection. After the Exodus, Jethro reunited Moses's family. A wise mentor, Jethro taught Moses to delegate the burden of settling many inevitable conflicts. This dedicated father and daughter devoted themselves to support God's call on the man whose stature as a towering moral figure in world history was exceeded only by Christ Jesus.

Puzzler: What foolishness led wise Jethro to offer his firstborn daughter to a foreign fugitive murderer? Centuries later the apostle Paul wrote, "God's foolishness is wiser than human wisdom, and God's weakness is stronger than human strength."[3] When have you watched examples of this sort of wise foolishness play out thus far in your lifetime?

King Saul and Michal: Princess Pawn of Politics

FD, Saul & Merab	HW, David & Michal	HW, Palti & Michal
FD, Saul & Michal	PP, David & singing women	PP, David & serving maids

Era: Kingdom

Story: 1 Samuel 16–19, 25:44; 2 Samuel 3:13–16, and 6. 1 Samuel traces King Saul's demented jealousy about David and ends with the deaths of Saul and all three of his sons in battle. 2 Samuel begins with the ensuing struggle for the throne among the twelve tribes of Israel.

Setting: The famous Ark of the Covenant held Israel's three treasured symbols: the golden urn holding manna recalling God's provision, Aaron's rod establishing the priestly line for God's worship; and the tablets of the Ten Commandments specifying God's law.[4] The capture of the Ark effected a despairing defeat and its return a joyful triumph.

The Ark stayed in the land throughout Saul's reign, but he disobeyed Samuel's orders to keep neither *any gain* in persons nor loot during a certain battle. Thus, God lifted favor from Saul and directed Samuel to anoint David secretly as the next king. But how was the young shepherd to prepare himself for his royal destiny? After all, rules govern who is and is not in the royal line, and he simply took care of his father's sheep. Meanwhile, the Philistines recruited the giant Goliath to challenge the Israelite army. The killer of Goliath would earn the king's daughter and royal perks. Or so it was promised. Hmm.

The rise of David to power makes the mouth of a playwright water. The corrosive thread of political ambition runs through dealings among King Saul, his younger daughter, Michal, and David. She is triangulated between loyalty to (and control by) her father and the dashing giant-killer, poet, harpist, and singer with whom she is in love. She is also aware that her father, in evil fits of jealousy, wants her to collude in killing the man about whom the women sing, "Saul has killed his thousands, and David his ten thousands." Upon the deaths of Saul and the heirs to the throne, David gains favor with tribe after tribe but not without strategic loss of blood, of which there are bucketloads in the struggle between David and Saul's house.

Michal's destiny is sealed in her choice between dispositions of jealousy over the throne from her father and joy over the Ark of the Covenant from her husband.

Puzzler: Moses would have turned over in his unknown grave at the cruel violations committed by Saul against his family, nation, and the LORD God. Today we tend to separate the leadership skills from the personal life and the religious practices of prominent people. What connections, if any, among these three habits of action does the author of 1 and 2 Samuel suggest?

Herod and the Daughter of Herodias [Salome]: Rivalry, Revelry, and Revenge

HW, Herod Philip I & Herodias	fd, Herod Antipas & [Salome]
FD, Herod Philip I & [Salome]	PP, John the Baptist & Herodias, [Salome]
HW, Herod Antipas & Herodias	

Era: Incarnation

Story: Mark 6:14–29; Matthew 14:1–12; Luke 3:1–20, 9:7–9, 13:31–35, 23:6–12.

Setting: Here's why children are not named Herod or Herodias. Herod the Great ruled as king from 37 to 4 BCE in Galilee and Judea. The Holy Family fled to Egypt to avoid his order to slaughter all baby boys in Bethlehem. About 20 BCE, he started building the Jerusalem Temple that Jesus knew. After his death, his three sons governed in the Jordan River region: Archelaus, Herod Antipas, and Herod Philip II the Tetrarch. When the Holy Family returned from Egypt, the brutal Archelaus ruled in Judea, so Joseph resided at Nazareth in Galilee where Antipas governed. This Herod built Tiberias and Sepphoris. Joseph may have worked at the latter city, not far from Nazareth. Herodias married two of her uncles, sons of Herod the Great by different mothers, dumping Philip I, the father of Salome, for Antipas. This self-protective stepfather stained sensuous Salome's soul with innocent blood. Salome married Philip II the Tetrarch. He enlarged Bethsaida and built Caesarea Philippi, where Peter confessed that Jesus was the Messiah. Herod Agrippa I, grandson of Herod the Great, ruled in 37–44 CE. He executed Jesus's disciple James and put Peter in prison. He died suddenly after he took glory to himself rather than to God. His son Herod Agrippa II ruled east of the Jordan. After hearing Paul's legal defense, he concluded that Paul had done nothing worthy of death or imprisonment but sent him to Rome to be tried by Caesar. There Paul wrote epistles safely under Roman guard.

Jesus called Herod Antipas a "fox." When Pilate sent Jesus to Herod to be questioned, Jesus would not speak to him. Speaking truth to power can be fatal—but not forever. Women following John the Baptist's message could call this childless man their father. Millions of boys and hundreds of churches have been named after "the voice of one crying out in the wilderness: 'Prepare the way of the Lord, make his paths straight.'"

Puzzler: The three Synoptic Gospels report Herod's disquiet about his execution of John the Baptist. He even believed that Jesus was John raised from the dead. Did he hope against all reason that John was not dead, or did he fear that John was coming back to retaliate? Did he want a second chance, or did he feel haunted by John's ghost? Finally, he met Jesus. Why did "gentle Jesus, meek and mild"[5] give Herod's uneasy conscience only a stony silence?

Philip and Four Daughters: An Evangelist Begets Prophets

PP, Philip & Hellenist women	PP, Paul & Philip's 4 daughters
FD, Philip & 4 daughters	PP, Agabus & Philip's 4 daughters

Era: Church

Story: Acts 6:1–7, 8:4–40, 21:8–16.

Setting: The Church formed quickly after the manifestation of the Holy Spirit at Pentecost. Thousands of Jewish pilgrims became believers and stayed on to receive daily teaching from the apostles. This new community shared their belongings to meet everyone's needs, especially those of widows. While the pilgrims spoke different languages, Greek was the official international language. But Hellenized (Greek-speaking) widows felt neglected at the meals where the Aramaic language predominated. The apostles chose seven godly Greek-speaking men as deacons to make sure these women were well served. Jews who saw believers in Jesus as a threat stoned the most famous deacon, Stephen, to death. Saul, a devout Jewish scholar, approved of this and scouted house to house to imprison believers. Persecution caused them to scatter far and wide. They kept spreading the good news of Jesus to fulfill his commission to go everywhere to preach, baptize, and teach. Meanwhile, Saul had a dramatic conversion and started preaching the Gospel to Gentiles. He changed his Jewish name to Paul. Including Gentiles in the church further fueled the hostility of traditionalist Aramaic-speaking Jews in Jerusalem.

One deacon, Philip the Evangelist, traveled north, south, and then northwest along the Mediterranean coast to preach, baptize, and teach in obedience to Jesus's last instructions. People responded eagerly to Philip's gifted ministry. Perhaps his sensitivity to widows' needs gave him skills to treat strangers with dignity, listen to them, put them at ease, and encourage them with the Gospel. Philip's use of Scripture spread joy like that of the couple from Emmaus.

His four daughters heard his stories of curious people he encountered. They learned how to interpret Scripture, speak concisely and convincingly, detect phoniness, introduce Jesus on the spur of the moment, surmount cultural differences, follow God's leading, call upon seasoned leaders when necessary, take into consideration a person's particular situation, and do all this with conviction and respect for God and others. That's what prophets do.

Puzzler: Despite knowing he would face trouble there, Paul headed back to Jerusalem to report on his missionary trips. In Caesarea, he stayed at Philip's house. Agabus, a prophet, graphically warned Paul, but we have no input from the four prophetic sisters. Why would these women have even been mentioned here, but not their words of prophetic wisdom? Paul went on anyway and lasted only seven days in Jerusalem until Rome took him into custody for years.

Supplemental Stories

Although not many stories about fathers and daughters appear in Scripture, they stand out for the decisive impact of this relationship for good or ill. The downfall of three tragic figures, Lot, Pharaoh, and King Saul, followed from failure to honor their daughters. But the faith of Job, Jethro, and Jairus gave the world a joyous heritage of transformation and restoration.

Caleb and Acsah
Era: Judges. Story: Joshua 15:13–19; Judges 1:11–15.
Faith-filled Caleb, the older of only two men to go from Egypt into the Promised Land, gave his daughter to a bold soldier and honored her request for a generous wedding gift.

Jephthah and Only Child
Era: Judges. Story: Judges 11:1—12:7.
Before this rejected half-brother in his family attacked the unwelcoming Ammonites, he made a rash and ungodly vow to the LORD. Family strife erupted into civil war.

Levite and a Woman from Bethlehem
Era: Judges. Story: Judges 19–21.
A woman ran away from a Levite man and returned home to Bethlehem, but her father returned her to the man. Abuse of women hit rock bottom in the rape and civil war that ensued.

Heman and Three Daughters
Era: Kingdom. Story: 1 Chronicles 25:1–8; 2 Chronicles 5; Psalm 88.
David established music guilds for worship. A prophet, instrumentalist, and music teacher, Heman, with his heirs, offered a lasting heritage for the Temple and Ark of the Covenant.

Shallum and Daughters
Era: Exile. Story: Nehemiah 3:6–12, 7:45; Ezra 2:42; 10:24.
Shallum, a gatekeeper, returned to Jerusalem from Exile and ruled a half-district during repair of its walls. Though he may have married a foreigner, his daughters loyally joined the effort.

Jairus and Only Child
Era: Incarnation. Story: Mark 5:21-43, Luke 8:40–56, Matthew 9:18–26.
Jephthah and Jairus form a stark contrast regarding their daughters. Jesus stepped into this scene of suffering and despair with healing in his hand and hem (see p. 106).

5

Mothers and Sons: Enduring Formation

Eve rejoiced, "I have produced a man with the help of the LORD."[1] Her words convey the first appreciative acknowledgement of God in the biblical story. Holding little baby Cain to her breast, "the mother of all living" recognized the wonder of new life from the Creator's hand via woman. Naturally the Bible reminds us that Adam was involved, too. However, by the time Adam beheld Cain, nine months of an organic ongoing connection of anticipation and nurture between Eve and Cain had already bound mother and child together. A mother notices the baby's first movement and thereafter rarely forgets that a new life is taking shape in her womb. The first sense to develop, hearing fills the baby's world with the steady and reliable heartbeat of the mother. We are still learning about factors that affect a child before birth. Whether shalom or tension, joy or apprehension, predominates as birth approaches makes a lasting difference.

Birth is by far the most traumatic thing that happens to a human body. Slowly and tediously, bouts of terrible squeezing force the baby out of the cushioned womb into a world absent the mother's reassuring heartbeat. The first intake of air into tiny lungs produces the scream that makes glad the hearts of onlookers. Then light assaults the infant's barely open eyes. The next rite of passage requires the infant to exercise sucking for nurture. It is a grace that we can't remember the most terrifying transition in our lives!

For the mother, birth begins the process of separation that will continue intensely for two decades and continues until death. What desperate faith led Jochebed to tuck her fine baby boy in a basket and relinquish him to the Nile River? How many years passed before Hannah told Samuel it was time for him to be responsible for his own cloaks? Breathes there a mother who feels adequately appreciated for hours of labor for her children during their inevitable pains and disappointments? Then how does a mother deal with the separation of her dreams and hopes from those of her adult children? Eve's cry of joy at Cain's birth came to grief. Yet mothers, devout or not, still hope for blessing from God's command to "be fruitful and multiply."

Even today mothers usually invest more in a child's crucial formative years than fathers. This enduring bond may bring about *de*formation as well as *re*formation. Both processes come from sustained presence and persistence for good or evil, as the examples to come show. Remember this. The future still belongs to those who have children.

Hagar and Ishmael: Meeting the Seeing and Hearing God

bs/HW, Abraham & Sarah	MS, Hagar & Ishmael	ms, Sarah & Ishmael
NM, Abraham & Hagar	MS, Sarah & Isaac	PP, Isaac & Hagar

Era: Founders

Story: Genesis 12:10—13:2, 15:1—18:15, 21:1–21, 25:12–18. See allegory, Galatians 4:21–31.

Setting: When two parties reached terms of peace, they would "cut a covenant" ceremonially. An animal was led between the two parties and cut in half. Both sides ate together from it, ensuring symbolically that no poison corrupted the treaty. Genesis 15 illustrates a dream-like or mystical enactment of cutting a covenant between the LORD and Abram. In this covenant God told Abram that his descendants would return after a period of slavery to live in this Promised Land. All males were to bear the physical sign of circumcision. As you know from chapter 2 above, Sarai's barrenness presented a problem. Nevertheless, God buttressed the covenant through *her* son by renaming the couple Abraham and Sarah.

When famine forced Abram and Sarai to go to Egypt for food, Abram attempted to dump beautiful Sarai on Pharaoh for a handsome price (see p. 68). An exchange of gifts was expected at the time of a marriage in ancient Egypt. The gifts could include jewelry, property, and livestock as well as servants. The couple may have obtained Hagar in such an exchange. Sarai and Abram took God's promise of a son into their own hands by using Hagar to conceive a child. Partly through her own pride, Hagar found Sarah intolerable and ran away. Hagar's Egyptian deities could not help her, but the LORD and Hagar *saw* each other. She obediently returned to Sarai to give birth to Ishmael. Partly through his own pride, Ishmael treated baby Isaac rudely. Like mother, like son. Finally, the renamed Sarah and Abraham joined forces and sent Hagar and Ishmael away. In the desert, the LORD *heard* their cries.

Despite the ill-treatment of her master and mistress, twice God provided for Hagar and promised the life of her son and many descendants. The first theophany, a visitation of deity in human form, came to a foreign discarded slave woman. She named the place "Well of the Living One who sees me." Jesus first revealed that he was Messiah to an outcast woman at a well.[2] Like Father, like Son. Both women received life-giving water.

Puzzler: Abraham, both of his sons, and all his male servants bore the physical sign of the covenant, but Abraham caved on the covenant by taking Sarah's solution over God's promise. Hagar (and her descendants) bore the brunt of the fallout. Nevertheless, God kept the covenant and honored Hagar's obedience. What is the true purpose of the covenant if those who receive it break it, yet others who don't receive it are blessed by it? See Romans 9:30–33.

Rebekah and Twin Sons: "The Elder Shall Serve the Younger"

HW, Isaac & Rebekah	HW, Esau & Judith, Basemath	HW, Esau & Mahalath
MS, Rebekah & Esau, Jacob	HW, Jacob & Leah, Rachel	MS, Rachel & Benjamin

Era: Founders

Story: Genesis 25:19—28:22, 32–35 (review chapters 29–31). Chapter 34 is featured below (p. 51). See also Hebrews 11:20, 12:16–17.

Setting: The city of Ur probably stood on the Euphrates River upstream from where the Tigris joined it to empty into the Persian Gulf. Terah had three sons, Abram, Nahor, and Haran. Haran, the father of Lot, died before Terah left Ur. The families of Terah, Abram, and Nahor set out northwest following the Euphrates toward its source and stopped at Haran. From Haran, Abram took Sarai with Lot and the servants southeast, where they met the Jordan River. They lived in the hills between the Jordan and the Mediterranean Sea. Nahor and his wife, Milcah, had eight sons. The eighth one, Bethuel, had at least two children, son Laban and daughter Rebekah.

After Sarah died, Rebekah agreed to travel to the land of Abraham to marry her cousin, Isaac, the son of promise and peacemaker (see p. 61). At last Rebekah conceived fraternal twins, Esau and Jacob, who began fighting in her womb. When she asked the LORD why she was in such misery, the answer offered a mystery. Two nations within her would divide; "the one shall be stronger than the other, the elder shall serve the younger."

Like Sarah, she tried to take this message into her own hands. But God's view of *strength* and *service* did not match Rebekah's. While Isaac favored Esau, the outdoorsman, the younger Jacob stayed quietly at home with mama. She manipulated for mastery over Esau and her husband, and Jacob colluded. The anger that Jacob roused forced him to flee to Laban, and you already know some of the trickery Laban pulled on Jacob (review p. 22). Rather than giving Jacob the upper hand over Esau, Rebekah's clever schemes caused the foretold division. The story never mentions her again. Jacob made it back home to Isaac, and together both twins buried him.

In a potent and counter-intuitive way, God's direct intervention brought a truce between the twins. Yet to this day, a cloud of suspicion and hostility hangs over their descendants.

Puzzler: God's way of fulfilling a prophecy usually catches us by surprise. For instance, despite specific details foretold concerning Messiah, few recognized that Jesus was he because they had a misconception of the Messiah's true mission. We tend to misconstrue prophecies and realize God's real intentions only in hindsight. So—in your opinion, which of the twins was the stronger, and in what way(s) did the elder Esau serve the younger Jacob?

Respecting Rizpah and Seven Palace Sons

NM, Saul & Rizpah	MS, Merab & 5 sons	PP, Ishbaal & Rizpah
MS, Rizpah & Armoni, Mephibosheth	PP, Abner & Rizpah	PP, David & Rizpah

Era: Kingdom

Story: 2 Samuel 3:6–12, 21:1–14.

Setting: Transfer of power commonly involves power struggles and bloodshed then and now in many parts of the world. After King Saul and his son Jonathan died in battle, the throne went up for grabs. Judah in the south quickly made David its king, and Joab commanded David's army. The northern tribes, especially Saul's Benjamite tribe, remained loyal to the house of Saul. Abner, the commander of Saul's army, made Ishbaal, another son of Saul, king over Israel. In such times, the ambitious and seditious employed a blatant power ploy by sleeping with one or more of the current or deceased king's concubines. Saul left behind at least one concubine and also a broken treaty with the Gibeonites, loyal servants in Israel since the era of the Judges.

In the long war between Saul's house and David's, David's grew stronger while Saul's became weaker. Then Ishbaal, probably testing the ambitions of Abner, falsely accused him of sleeping with Saul's concubine, Rizpah. The furious Abner decided to go over to David's side and brought Israel with him. David welcomed him in good faith with a celebration. However, without cell phones or Internet for news updates from David, Joab encountered Abner and stabbed him for having killed his brother in battle. David publicly mourned Abner. During more violent deaths, David kept smelling like a rose and eventually won Israel in the north.

During a famine, the LORD reminded David of Saul's broken treaty with the Gibeonites. For expiation, they asked for Saul's five grandsons by his older daughter, Merab, and the two sons of Rizpah by Saul. David (gleefully?) permitted the Gibeonites to wipe out the remaining contenders for the throne from Saul's house. The seven impaled bodies were left to the elements, but the famine continued for a third year. After Rizpah conducted a compelling protest, David gave the bones not only of Saul and Jonathan but also those of the seven a respectful burial. "After that, God heeded supplications for the land." The rains fell from heaven.

Rizpah, a bona fide mother in the kingdom, spoke truth to power without a word.

Puzzler: People love David, the singing, slinging shepherd/poet/king, and the man after God's heart. So Rizpah, a mere concubine of Saul who dared to bare David's darker side in his rise to power, receives scant attention. However, we know the names of her sons while those of Princess Merab's sons are lost to history. Which side of the battle for the throne did Rizpah serve, Saul's house or David's house, or neither or both? What kindled her protest?

Bathsheba and Solomon: Looking Out for Number Two

HW, Uriah & Bathsheba	MS, Bathsheba & Solomon	PP, Adonijah & Bathsheba
NM/HW, David & Bathsheba	PP, David & Abishag	PP, Adonijah & Abishag
PP, Nathan & Bathsheba		PP, Solomon & Abishag

Era: Kingdom

Story: 2 Samuel 12:9–25; 1 Kings 1–2; 1 Chronicles 17, 22; Matthew 1:6.

Setting: Ancient Israel practiced division of power in three distinct roles of prophet, priest, and king. When mutually bound together but without overlap, these offices protected and supported God's covenant. Kings took economic, judicial, and military responsibilities. Prophets focused on communicating God's Word and applying divine directives in current situations. Priests conducted worship by leading prayers, singing praises, celebrating feasts, offering sacrifices, and overseeing other rites and rituals. Carved horns on the four corners of the huge altar at the entrance to the tent of the LORD symbolized the strength of atoning peace between God and the nation. Priests put blood of burnt sacrifices on the four horns. People seeking sanctuary grasped them in a concrete gesture of casting themselves upon God's protection.

The notorious backstory of this family's situation comes up in chapter 8 below. Here the focus turns to Bathsheba's number two child, Solomon, by her number two husband, David. The LORD loved the king's last son like a father. This son mirrored David's selection to be king as the youngest of eight sons.[3] David prepared for Solomon to replace the tent with a grand Temple for the LORD. But Adonijah, the son next in line, announced his ascent to the throne. Soliciting Bathsheba's help, the *prophet* Nathan quickly reminded the elderly *king* to name his successor. David immediately summoned the *priest* Zadok, and the three offices harmoniously transferred power to Solomon with no bloodshed—for the moment.

God kept David from building the Temple because of the blood he had spilled in his rise to power and his reign thereafter. He also left related posthumous business for Solomon to finish off despite the assumed sanctuary at the horns of the altar. Queen Mother Bathsheba bent to Solomon's astute will on related matters of state.

"Solomon" sounds similar to "Shalom." Solely by God's grace, Solomon reigned in peace, and the people enjoyed the blessings of the Golden Age of Israel.

Puzzler: David passed over older sons to favor his youngest and last son, Solomon, born to Bathsheba, who had been the wife of Uriah. God's Law required adulterers, both the man and the woman, to be stoned to death.[4] But then and now God does not despise "a broken and contrite heart."[5] What does Solomon's name suggest about his parents and about God?

Elizabeth and John the Baptist: Forerunners in Their DNA

HW, Zechariah & Elizabeth	PP, John & Mary	PP, John & Herodias, Salome
MS, Elizabeth & John	PP, Zechariah & Mary	

Era: Incarnation

Story: Malachi 4:5–6; Luke 1, 3, Matthew 1:18–25, Mark 6:14–29 (see pp. 4, 38).

Setting: Dr. Luke traveled with St. Paul, including time in Ephesus. There he could have met Mary at the home of Jesus's disciple John to hear her story. A couple entering the legal bonds of betrothal were considered husband and wife even though no sexual relations took place during this preparation period. Breaking a betrothal required a divorce proceeding and often besmirched the reputation of one or more in the family. A wife without children faced condemnation, ridicule, and disgrace, for she must have lost favor with God. Biblical angels principally deliver messages directly from God's throne. The sudden appearance of these mighty beings strikes us humans with fear, but courage and confidence follow in the wake of their departure.

Gabriel's message left Mary willing but stunned. His parting words, "For nothing will be impossible with God," still left concerns. What would become of her betrothal to Joseph? God had already prepared the spot-on person to whom she could go. Gabriel gently mentioned Mary's elderly relative Elizabeth, who was pregnant miraculously. On the trip, all of this reverberated in Mary's mind. When prenatal John gave a kick-start to Elizabeth's rapturous greeting, Mary burst into the Magnificat, the most widely sung hymn of praise in history. The whole scene basks in the empowering presence of the Holy Spirit. Perhaps this was the actual moment of Jesus's conception. For the next three months Mary was steeped in the elderly couple's hospitality and counsel. At John's birth, God opened the old priest's lips with the fifth message of expectant joy in Luke 1. He rightly proclaimed his son's destiny, but neither the one they expected nor the one Herod imposed. Meanwhile, the LORD's angel had solved the betrothal issue. As forerunners, Elizabeth prepared Mary for Jesus, and John prepared the world for Jesus.

Luke's account highlights two devoted mothers who, despite personal disgrace and the unjust deaths of their sons, *knew* that God's favor and mercy rested upon them. Hear Job clapping. The One for whom nothing is impossible keeps promises and gives joy.

Puzzler: Through the pages of the biblical story walk many characters who appear at a momentous point to do an essential task for which they are uniquely equipped. Then they disappear. Both Elizabeth and John the Baptist fit the description. When have you been a recipient of such a gift at a crucial point in your life OR offered your gift to someone at a turning point in his or her life? As you relive that event, what does it mean to you now?

Mary and Jesus: Seeking First the Kingdom of God

HW, Joseph & Mary	PP, shepherds & Mary	PP, Simeon & Mary	PP, John & Mary
MS, Mary & Jesus	PP, wise men & Mary	PP, Jesus & Anna	PP, Luke & Mary

Era: Incarnation

Stories: *Birth narratives*: Matthew 1:18—2:23 (prophecies: Isaiah 7:14; Micah 5:2; Hosea 11:1; Jeremiah 31:15; "Nazorean" means "despised," Psalm 22:6; Isaiah 53:3) and Luke 1:26—2:52.
Ministry of Jesus: John 2:1–11. See also stories featuring Mary (review pp. 4, 26, 60).
Precedence of mission over family: Matthew 10:34–39; Luke 12:51–53, 14:25–27, 18:29–30.
Redefinition of family: Matthew 12:46–50; Mark 3:31–35; Luke 8:19–21, 11:27–28.
Rejection based on Jesus's family: Matthew 13:53–58; Mark 6:1–6; John 6:35–44.
At the cross: John 19:25–27. *In the Church*: Acts 1:14.

Setting: During his travels with Paul, Dr. Luke, himself a Greek, was compiling an account of Jesus's life because many eyewitnesses of Jesus had now died. Martyrs included John's brother, James. Picture Luke and John reviewing Luke's accumulation of notes while Paul taught for months in Ephesus. Luke's heart leaped with anticipation of meeting Mary, whom Jesus had entrusted to John's care. Would the elderly woman's story match birth tales of Roman and Greek gods familiar to Luke? Might the time be right for her to entrust to this Gentile secrets she had long pondered in her heart? Come, Holy Spirit.

Of all the Gospel writers, Luke records the most about Mary. Themes of rejection, distancing, and redefinition run through Jesus's interactions with his mother: "Did you not know that I must be in my Father's house?"; "Woman, what concern is that to you and to me?"; "Whoever comes to me and does not hate father and mother ... and even life itself, cannot be my disciple"; "No one who has left ... parents ... for the sake of the kingdom of God who will not get back very much more in this age, and in the age to come eternal life"; and it is not wombs and breasts that define motherhood but rather to "hear the word of God and obey it!"[6] Mary heard and obeyed despite the sword that pierced her soul. Yet the two closest to Jesus, his mother and John, received his last request and nurtured the early church.

Puzzler: The course of true love takes many bumps, yet love "bears all things, believes all things, hopes all things, endures all things."[7] Luke recorded that Mary's destiny began with an angel's visit, and Jesus's agony concluded with an angel's visit. Compare the words they said in their moments of greatest devotion (1:38b, 22:42b). Like mother, like son. Put their words in your own words and apply them to a current concern in your life. See what happens.

Supplemental Stories

The enduring influence of mothers for *re*formation or *de*formation grows *more* acute when children grow up in father-absent homes. Sentimental symbolism often associated with motherhood is *less* representative when more women than men forsake marriage. Observe the direction in which these mothers and sons were headed within the four degrees of love.

Sarah and Isaac
Era: Founders. Story: Genesis 17:15—18:15, 21:1–21 (see also Galatians 4:21–31).
Note: Paul's use of Sarah and Hagar for an allegory does not endorse the behavior of any character in the story. What direction is suggested by Sarah's first and second laughs?

Mother and Micah
Era: Judges. Story: Judges 17–18.
See what happens here when the complementary roles of prophet, priest, and king get mixed up and out of whack. How does the mother reflect the disorder of the times?

Two Mothers and Sons
Era: Kingdom. Story: 1 Kings 3:10–28.
Solomon, often cited as the wisest man who ever lived, meets a challenge in the legal case presented by two prostitutes. What do you think of the outcome the author points out?

Two Royal Mothers and Each's Son, Abijah, and Asa
Era: Kingdom. Story: 1 Kings 14:1–18, 15:1–15.
When Jeroboam (of Israel) rebelled against King Rehoboam (of Judah) to split the kingdom, parallel ruptures followed in each royal family. Which mother would you rather be?

The Mother of Rufus and Paul
Era: Church. Story: Romans 16:13 (see also Mark 15:21).
Consider the backstory of this connection and its significance for Paul. Imagine how this spiritual mother of Paul might have told him about her husband's encounter with Jesus.

Lois, Eunice and Timothy
Era: Church. Story: Acts 16:1–5; 2 Timothy 1:1–14.
This spiritual father honors two women who raised up a future pastor/teacher for the church. What factors made Timothy a key player in the mission to the Gentiles?

6

Brothers and Sisters: Bloodline and Bloodshed

Of the three family connections between the two genders, we are likely to enjoy least the fact that we did not choose our brothers and sisters, at least during the years we share a house with them. Not only the protection of an older sibling from an admiring younger sibling but also the inevitable squabbles over turf or perceived injustices fertilize seeds of love and hate in our hearts. Loyalty and rivalry can erupt within seconds of each other, creating an intense mix of episodes that tax the energies of even the wisest parents. While only children enjoy some advantages, they must depend upon cousins, friends, and neighbors to fill the gap left by the absence of siblings. Interactions among siblings forged in the crucible of 24/7 life together present fertile ground for our ongoing development of self-awareness, identification of emotions, and recognition of potency.

The influence of siblings begins early in life before we have the vocabulary to name what is happening externally and internally. In later life, especially after the deaths of our parents, few others have a longer history with us than our siblings. Yet our memories may still differ so much from each other that we wonder if we did really did grow up in the same house. Extended interactions with siblings and their stories broaden our understanding of self and others.

What did God have in mind for us in our dealings with siblings? The Bible offers the fewest stories in this category of relationships between the genders. However, the Old and New Testaments give us two extraordinary examples of sibling dynamics respectively: Miriam, Aaron, and Moses (one girl, two boys) and Lazarus, Martha, and Mary (one boy, two girls). In both cases, these siblings transcended their own interests to move God's Grand Story into the salvific events of the Exodus and Passion of Christ.

A longing for trustworthy community founded in the family brings us the best of civilization and the invention of methods of keeping in touch that make the world smaller and less lonely. However, you will also see examples in this chapter of siblings operating *outside* God's ways. Betrayal of trust among siblings may bring disastrous results on individuals and the family's legacy. Collective sibling ardor can result in vicious and deadly tribalism.

Human beings need more than all else to be adopted into the life of the Holy Trinity. Jesus is the firstborn brother in a new family of those given the power to become sons and daughters of God. Members of the early church continually referred to each other as brothers and sisters. The Church's call remains to welcome God's kingdom on earth as in heaven by honoring God first and living honorably with our siblings in Christ. Together we bear the image of God.

Laban and Rebekah: Living for the Bottom Line

PP, servant & Rebekah	PP, servant & Deborah, maids	HW, Jacob & Rachel, Leah
FD, Bethuel & Rebekah	HW, Isaac & Rebekah	FD, Laban & Leah, Rachel
BS, Laban & Rebekah	MS, Rebekah & Esau, Jacob	nm, Jacob & Bilhah, Zilpah
HW, Esau & Mahalath	HW, Esau & Judith, Basemath	FD, Jacob & Dinah, sisters

Era: Founders

Story: Genesis 24–32, especially 24, 26:34—29:30, 30:25—32:31 (skim intermediate passages). Note also Genesis 35:8, 46:6–7, and 49:29–31.

Setting: Jacob's wealth came from interventions from God and his own schemes. God gave Jacob a dream in which animals with the recessive genes for speckles, spots, and streaks would breed with each other, but in waking reality they might present the plain coat of the dominant gene. Jacob's breeding methods appear superstitious to modern city dwellers, but this requires a closer look. Jacob peeled and stripped the sticks of poplar, almond, and Oriental plane (probably chestnut or sycamore) to expose the tannins in the bark. Herbal medicines in these sticks could help with urogenital problems, reduce fevers, work as anti-inflammatories, aid in reducing reproductive disorders, and more.[1] Ewes could eat the sticks and drink the water in which the nutrients had dissolved in the hot sun. Therefore, these animals would be healthier and more likely to produce more and healthier lambs. Jacob added these herbal treatments *only* when stronger animals were simultaneously feeding and breeding. Voilà, wealth!

Not that the trickster deserved such blessing. Laban gave Jacob several bitter tastes of his own medicine. Rebekah and Laban came from a family in which deception and subterfuge were normative, especially when such endeavors increased one's privilege, power, or wealth. In the end, Jacob wrestled with the consequences of his ploys until he was forced to beg God for a blessing. Yet the deceptions of his sons who followed his example ravaged him for years.

For us, these biblical stories rise above the warnings of cautionary tales because God's Grand Story leads to reformation. We have no reports of Jacob lying again.

Puzzler: All of us meet people like Rebekah and Laban. From your life experiences and wisdom, note ways you might "set the characters straight" along the way. How might you warn them of potential trouble, prevent it, address it, and neutralize its effect? Take into account God's role in the story and the degree of sensitivity to God on the part of the characters. Review point #8 on the dog-eared page (p. xvi). How exactly does God play the role of hero here?

The Brothers of Dinah: Travesty and Tragedy

FD, Jacob & Dinah	PP, Hamor & Dinah	PP, Hivites & Dinah
NM, Shechem & Dinah	BS, Simeon, Levi & Dinah	BS, Leah's other sons & Dinah

Era: Founders

Story: Genesis 34. See also insights from Genesis 10:15–20, 30:21, 46:15, 49:5–7; Joshua 9; 1 Kings 9:20. Hivites are sometimes labeled Shechemites and Gibeonites.

Setting: In order of appearance in the record, the following terms of the covenant with the LORD were incumbent upon Abraham: obey by changing his location; be a blessing to nations nearby and beyond; raise his promised son by Sarah and their descendants to keep the covenant; take possession of the Promised Land (by peaceful means likely to bless and be a blessing); circumcise all males as a sign of the covenant; and name the promised son Isaac, which means "laughter." The LORD promised Abraham he would live a long life and be buried here. Even though his descendants would live in oppression elsewhere, they would return one day. Great nations numbering like the stars would call Abraham and Sarah father and mother.

Centrally placed in and central to the terms of the covenant came this reality. "[Abraham] believed the LORD; and the LORD reckoned it to him as righteousness" (Genesis 15:6). Sounds good, but trace in this story what actually happened in regard to the covenant. The honorable Hivite, Prince Shechem, fell in love with Leah's daughter Dinah, and told her so. He sent Hamor to Jacob in good faith to offer generous terms for marriage. Not only no hint of coercion but also no hint of the LORD passed between the families. This process bears some resemblance to our culture's current endorsement of consensual sexual relations, except that now a marriage is not necessarily expected. The reprehensible response of her brothers made flagrantly fraudulent use of religion to betray their neighbor's good will. The stench lingered generations later.

Ignoring the centrality of *belief* desecrated the covenant. Ongoing degradation of the covenant ran parallel with corrosion of respect for a woman's will regarding a husband. It starts downhill with Rebekah, compounds with Leah and Rachel, and dives to abhorrence with Dinah. Yet Judah, as we have seen, thought little of using the services of a prostitute while Reuben expected to get away with sleeping with his father's concubine. God and Jacob did not forget.

Puzzler: Dinah's brothers thought Shechem "had committed an outrage *in Israel* by lying with Jacob's daughter, *for such a thing ought not to be done*" (both emphases mine). In your opinion, why or why not? In Christianity, there are two covenants, Holy Baptism and Holy Matrimony. Consider how belief in the covenant with God parallels belief in exclusiveness in the marriage covenant. It harks back to the leave and cleave clause in Genesis 2:24.

Aaron, Moses, and Miriam: Unbroken Threefold Cord

HW, Amram & Jochebed	ms, princess & Moses	HW, Moses & Cushite wife
MS, Jochebed & baby boy	HW, Moses & Zipporah	BS, Aaron & Miriam
BS, baby boy & Miriam		PP, Aaron & Cushite woman

Era: Exodus

Story: Exodus 1:1—2:10, 4:10—5:5, 6:13—8:19, 15:1–21, 17:8–16. Skim intermediate passages and the rest of Exodus, stopping to read chapters 28, 32, and 40. See also Numbers 12; Micah 6:1–8.

Setting: Each of the previous chapters refresh stories of this family in the transition from slavery to freedom (p. 12), a crisis in sibling dynamics (p. 20), and Jethro's role as a father figure for Moses (p. 36). Contemporary law codes in surrounding nations favored the rich over the poor, male over female, elder over younger, and master over servant. The Hebrews' experience in slavery profoundly altered their codes under God's Law. Miriam's and Zipporah's prominent roles in the direction of Moses's life also contributed to respect for women in their laws. Cush ran along the Red Sea toward the source of the Nile River, roughly current Ethiopia. The word means "black," indicating people of darker skin than the Egyptians and Hebrews.

After two unhappy stories, we need a joy break once again. After the chaotic dysfunction of the Founders' era and centuries of slavery away from the land of their ancestors, the Hebrews cried out to God for relief. Hope came in the faith of a family that would defy Pharaoh to the end. This family hung together in ways unknown in Genesis. Miriam cunningly stepped up to the plate to watch over her tiny baby brother adrift in the Nile while her mother, Jochebed, kept watch over three-year-old Aaron. The princess paid Jochebed to nurse *their* shared son.

The stuttering Moses joined forces with eloquent Aaron to confront Pharaoh, and Miriam led the people in song and dance to celebrate their freedom from slavery. However, the three siblings squabbled over crucial matters of worship and leadership that could have derailed the fledgling nation. Pay special attention to how they remained an unbroken threefold cord.[2] In the Hebrew Scriptures, no story more expressly marks the Lord God as the mighty hero.

Puzzler: Under God's directives, Moses reformed the people's identity from slaves in Egypt to worshippers of the Lord God who delivered them from Pharaoh. Laws put boundaries on who and what would and would not be allowed among them. Reflect upon the two major controversies, one led primarily by the priest Aaron (Exodus 32) and the other by the prophet Miriam (Numbers 12). Consider the seriousness of these two sibling spats and their respective resolutions.

Absalom and Tamar: Rape and Revenge

BS, Absalom & Tamar	PP, Jonadab & Tamar	bs/NM, Amnon & Tamar
FD, David & Tamar	PP, Amnon's servant & Tamar	

Era: Kingdom

Story: 2 Samuel 13. Backstory: 3:1–5.

Setting: Over the centuries, racy struggles for power in royal households have provided fodder for fiction and non-fiction. Kings, as well as wealthy and powerful men, amassed both wives and concubines whose hard work presented meals, clothing, and well-kept houses for multiple half-siblings. Solomon, David's son, had an unimaginable harem of 700 wives and 300 concubines.[3] The fugitive David married two women, not counting the estranged Michal, Saul's childless daughter. During David's early reign solely in Judah, he had six wives, and each had a son in the royal line of succession in the following birth order: Amnon, Kileab, Absalom, Adonijah, Shephatiah, and Ithream. Kileab, David's son by the widow Abigail, had lower pureblood status. Now predict the hot spot for succession to the throne.

Despite all David's winning characteristics, he utterly failed to discipline his sons. Possible causes are found in chapter 8 below, where connected stories will be unpacked in greater detail. Consider these givens: unruly male hormones, undulating adolescent emotions, a teenager's appetite, spoiled rich youth lacking supervision, a gorgeous half-sister with a bully brother, a colluding buddy, and a complicit servant—combined with lawful anticipation of becoming a king who can make up his own rules to get his own way with power to reward and punish as he wills. No doubt about it, here comes a scenario for inevitable disaster.

Absalom's eye was on the throne. Only a naïve person would cite rebuffed matrimony as the *only* cause of vengeance, and the brothers' crass cruelty as *merely* aggregate indifference to Tamar. Only a heartless person could read Tamar's words in this narrative and not grasp the intensity of her objections and a measure of her grief. Repeated here from Dinah's story, we find: "... such a thing is not done in Israel ... ." Beware of hooligans in high places.

Puzzler: In chapter 8, we will see this story's backstory and ending. It is too early to draw many conclusions. The exercises under "Concentrate" on the dog-eared page (p. xvi) ask you to identify with someone of the other gender. For men, how might Tamar have handled the situation differently? For women, which brother (half or full) acted worse? If one goal of God's Grand Story is to make us loathe that which is evil, to what degree does this story work in God's favor?

Jesus and Family Sisters: The Perfect Brother

bs, Jesus & sisters	bs, Jesus & women in Appendix B

Era: Incarnation

Story: Matthew 13:53–58; Mark 6:1–6.

Setting: It is hard to remember that the Bible is preeminently *God's* Grand Story. As many questions as I have about what became of characters such as Ishmael, Dinah, Laban, Tamar (both of them), the other sons of David, Rizpah, Jeremiah, Esther, Daniel, the woman at the well at Sychar, Lazarus, and many more, the Bible is *not their story*. Yet it seems a mistake that we don't know why Joseph disappears, and Jesus's sisters are mentioned only in passing at one event. We know Jesus's brothers did not believe in him until after the Resurrection, but we don't know that his sisters did not believe in him. The 120 at Pentecost included "certain women, including Mary the mother of Jesus, as well as his brothers." His brother James became the head of the early church in Jerusalem[4] and wrote the book that bears his name. The book of Jude may have been written by another brother. That's all the New Testament has to say about the half-siblings of Jesus. Perhaps that is because he widened his family to include all those who received him. As John's Gospel proclaims (1:12–13), these people were empowered to become sons and daughters of God.

I suggest two ways to approach the esteem in which Jesus held his sisters. First, select stories in Appendix B, listing women Jesus knew. He loved them, and they loved him. Not one story of Jesus with a woman derides her sexuality or presents her derogatorily. No man in history surpassed him in affirmation of women's faith, discipleship, commitment, and character. Because these sisters appear with Jesus in the Gospels, they are forever famous.

Second, read Jesus's paired proximate parables in which he identified with what mattered to men and women, especially the Lost Sheep and the Lost Coin, Luke 15:4–10; and the Ten Bridesmaids and Five Talents, Matthew 25:1–30. In the *only* parable about both genders, the Widow and the Unjust Judge, Luke 18:2–8, he affirmed the prayers of people who seek justice and hunger for godly mutuality reflecting the image of God.

Puzzler: To what extent and in what situations have you seen people mirror how they treat siblings at home with others outside the home? Do siblings generally treat each other better or worse, with more or less respect, than those outside the family? For only children who had no siblings or for those whose siblings were the same gender as theirs: who has been like the sister or brother you never had and has helped you to appreciate the other gender?

King Herod Agrippa II and Bernice: Upstaged by Jesus

BS/[NM], King Agrippa II & Bernice	PP, Festus & Bernice	PP, Paul & Bernice

Era: Church

Story: Acts 25:13—26:32. The backstory for Paul's arrest at the Temple and defenses before the Jewish Sanhedrin and Roman Governors Felix and Festus is in Acts 21:17—25:12.

Setting: Under Roman law, a person could not be put to death without the opportunity to speak before a judge and the accusers. A Roman governing official had to consent to any execution. Roman citizens could refuse to go before a local provincial court and could appeal to a higher court all the way to Caesar. They were spared degrading punishments like being beaten with rods, scourging, and crucifixion. Citizenship came by (1) birth in a Roman family, (2) purchase at a high price, or (3) outstanding service to Rome. King Agrippa II (see p. 38) was an expert on Jewish beliefs and laws, their Messianic hope, and the threat followers of Jesus posed to Jewish officials. As king, he controlled Temple finances and could appoint the high priest from the Sadducees, who did not believe in life after death, a comforting belief for tyrants. The course of true love evaded Bernice, the oldest daughter of King Herod Agrippa I. She was married at age 13 to her uncle Herod of Chalcis and had two sons. After his death, she lived with her brother, Agrippa II. To foil rumors of incest, she married Polemon, King of Cilicia, but soon returned to her brother. Sometime after the events in this story, Titus, son of Emperor Vespasian, took her as mistress but paid little attention to her.

Paul had appealed to Caesar, but Festus had no charge to bring to Caesar's attention. Since King Agrippa II had been in office several years, Festus sought his opinion on the matter. When the royal siblings paid the official welcome visit to the new governor Festus, Bernice likely knew of the respect Jesus had given women and was curious to meet Paul.

The pomp of the siblings slowly melted at the impact of the risen Jesus Christ on Paul. Note what happened. Festus lost his composure at Paul's call to repentance. Furthermore, Paul challenged the king, "Do you believe the prophets? I know that you believe." About Bernice, we know only she agreed that Paul did not deserve death. Paul's appeal to Caesar enabled them to pass the buck to the emperor. Lord, have mercy.

Puzzler: The Gospels devote a large proportion of their accounts to Jesus's trials in the last week of his life, known as Holy Week and the Passion. Luke's account in Acts covers Paul's hearings extensively. In both cases, why did officials break their own laws? Who can be trusted here: Paul, the Roman officials, the religious officials accusing Paul, you, me, or no one? At this point, what would you want to ask Paul and Jesus about their actions and words?

Supplemental Stories

Often historians and authors depict winners and losers, but readers delight when the best part of the story reveals a reversal of these expectations in the end. The Bible revels in the least, the lost, and the last whom God raises up as victors over villains. Take note in this regard that siblings, whether allies or rivals, exert distinctive propensities for nobleness and vengeance.

Nebaioth and Mahalath
Era: Founders. Story: Genesis 25:12–16, 26:34–35, 27:41—28:9.
When Esau's wives embittered Isaac and Rebekah, she stoked this hostility to Jacob's advantage. Esau appeased with a third wife, the sister of Ishmael's firstborn. Politics!

Rahab & Brothers
Era: Exodus. Story: Joshua 2, 6 (skim 5, 7); see also Matthew 1:5; Hebrews 11:31.
During siege, young men led the offense, but in faith, Rahab had worked a deal to save her family. Her brothers acquiesced. Her scarlet cord endures as a symbol of God's salvation.

Job and Sisters
Eras: Founders (oral tradition); Kingdom (wisdom literature). Story: Job 1–2, and 42.
During Job's trials, his family of origin never shows up, but in the end, they rejoice with him. Job, the righteous family man, graciously accepts his sisters' tokens of tardy apologies.

Ahaziah and Jehoshabeath
Era: Kingdom. Story: 2 Chronicles 21:1—23:21 or 2 Kings 8:16–29, and 11.
Their paternal grandfather was good Jehoshaphat, King of Judah in the royal line of David. Their maternal grandfather was wicked Ahab, King of Israel. Whose line would prevail?

Paul and Sister
Era: Church. Story: Acts 22:30—23:35.
She taught family and civil loyalty to her observant young son. He saved innocent lives from violent death by his vigilance in taking timely action on information he intercepted. Kudos!

Paul and Deaconess Phoebe, Apostle Junia
Era: Church. Story: Romans 16:1–16 *especially verses 1–2, 7.*
Language distinguishing blood-related sisters from spiritual sisters is absent in this list of co-laborers. Only Jesus surpasses Paul in the count of women they encountered and esteemed.

The Tutorial Reviewed

While we do not choose our parents, children, and siblings, it is equally important to recognize that human conception never happens unconsciously. Whether or not conception is *desired*, either both parties of normal mental capacity knowingly consent to the action required for it to happen, or it comes about by rape. Tragically, not all children are wanted. This truth imposes moral obligations upon the man and woman or boy and girl whose action results in conception. Their child is not an accident. Communities vary in responses to conflicted situations. In the end, the just and merciful God rules on the response of parents, child, *and* their community.

While the Bible *de*scribes roles for fathers and mothers, it does not *pre*scribe the roles issuing from their union. At home, internal and external concerns recommend collaboration and division of labor between parents. In the biblical examples given to us, fathers made crucial decisions that cast light or shadow over their children's lives. Through day-to-day presence, mothers wielded a lasting impact on their children's character. Remember that God does not prescribe these specific roles for a father or mother respectively. Single parents have a distinct disadvantage in being the lone maker of a myriad of both critical and inconsequential decisions. While grandparents, extended family members, teachers, coaches, and others can make a crucial difference in a child's life, the impact of father, mother, and siblings cannot be underestimated. Responsible community leaders pay close attention to these concerns.

The family tends the ground where seeds of faith, hope, and love may flourish or fail. Blessed be the sanctuary, be it humble or palatial, where every family member learns from errors and increases in wisdom and in stature, and in divine and human favor as Samuel and Jesus did.[1] Such a family points us further up and further into the four degrees of love of God and self. Nevertheless, family of origin does not irreversibly determine a person's character. Even identical twins can turn out quite differently. For good or ill, countless children have broken generational patterns, often encouraged by a person or group who chose to invest time and energy in them. Sometimes God directly intervenes to change the course of a life. Only God knows why, and only God judges with absolute trustworthiness and mercy.

Finally, may I venture a Golden Rule corollary for siblings taking the road to forgiveness, repentance, and sibling solidarity with our elder Brother Jesus? Sisters, treat a boy the way you would want your brother to be treated by a girl. Brothers, treat a girl the way you would want your sister to be treated by a boy. For next we turn to the magnificent peaks and mysterious potholes on a bumpy path, namely, Boy Meets Girl.

PART III

SEXUAL UNION: COVENANT, CONTRACT, AND CONCUPISCENCE

A certain bishop warned couples at the altar that marriage is an unnatural act which carries within it the seeds of divorce.[1] Therefore, the liturgy for blessing holy matrimony of necessity implores God's help when HE and SHE become WE, one flesh from two categorically different persons. Nevertheless, "love is strong as death, passion fierce as the grave ... Many waters cannot quench love, neither can floods drown it. If one offered for love all the wealth of one's house, it would be utterly scorned."[2]

Such nuptial hopes inspire poetry. Song of Solomon[3] sparkles like the diamond of an engagement ring and envisions the pearl of great price. The Beloved and Lover exchange exquisite expressions of love. Witnesses chime in to sing choruses. The spiritual mystery and corporal delight of erotic love arouse agony and ecstasy, separation and anticipation, yearning and yielding. The *covenant* celebrated here emanates from the inseparable Holy Trinity. Song of Solomon contrasts unequivocally with the exploitative trade of pornography.

Four times in Song of Solomon, the Lover calls the Beloved "my *sister*, my bride" and a fifth time "my *sister*, my love, my dove, my perfect one." The Beloved says of him, "O that you were like a *brother* to me, who nursed at my mother's breast!"[4] Not a hint of incest resides here. These bonds connote unreserved welcome and familial commitment. This couple will practice the precepts and priorities, loyalty and mutuality, that undergird their marriage. Their children will learn the meaning of faith, hope, and love from them.

The irony of Solomon's name calls up his 700 wives. Keeping track of the terms of so many marriages by *contract* for political and profitable liaisons must have been a legal nightmare. In the end, his divided loyalties eroded fidelity to the LORD God of Abraham, Leah, Moses, and Hannah. His lust also destined 300 concubines to servitude in his harem. This urge ignited by "the desire of the flesh, the desire of the eyes, the pride in riches"[5] is named *concupiscence*. In Song of Solomon I imagine the king's wistful envy of a rustic shepherd groom taking the hand of a lovely vine dresser in marriage. The devotion of this bride and groom sparkles still.

The stories featured in the next two chapters explore sexual liaisons with and without benefit of promises witnessed before God and community. Human promises can waver, but be prepared for unexpected entrances of divine action at unlikely places.

7

Recognized Marriage: Husbands and Wives

Part II examined connections within the family of origin that none of us choose. These forced choices actually serve to direct us toward decisions about what kind of person we would or would not want to live with if we had the choice. Today in much of the West, young people of legal age are permitted to decide about marriage, its alternatives, and gender. However, in the scope of human history, the latter is an innovation. Our current fascination with alternatives to marriage and sexual identity renders the terms "husband" and "wife" outdated or redefined. However, after we have exhausted, and been exhausted by, the experimentation of the sexual revolution, I predict that "husband" and "wife" will remain essential terms. Societies cannot be sustained without prudent definition and regulation of domestic matters.

God regulates, too. As early as Genesis 2:24, God establishes marriage and sets it apart from all other affiliations. A man leaves his parents to establish a bond with a woman to whom he clings faithfully in a physical union that bespeaks a broader unity of intents and purposes for their life together. Covenants figure prominently in this book because of their importance to the biblical authors. They repeatedly use marriage as a metaphor for God's covenant with people who believe. From Old Testament times through today, God's faithfulness to the Jewish people is nothing short of a historical miracle, enduring even when they had no land or government to support their identity. The New Testament echoes the Genesis passage and enriches it with the analogy of Christ and the Church.[1] Ponder these connections between God and marriage. Do people project on God the unity they feel when they fall in love or did God establish marriage to draw people into the unity of the Holy Trinity? What other spiritual factors apply?

Now take a deep breath. What roles are assigned to a husband and a wife in the Bible? King Lemuel's mother instructed him on this matter. He was probably weighing a decision about marriage or envisioning the qualities essential for his queen. Proverbs concludes with his mother's wisdom. After reading verses 10–31 in the final chapter, try this out. Replace "wife" with "husband" and "woman" with "man," and change the pronouns throughout accordingly. In verse 30 replace "beauty is" with "good looks are." Now read the revised version to an unsuspecting man and ask his opinion of this job description for husbands.

In this chapter, two sections compare how two couples dealt with their situations. I hope that the commonalities and contrasts suggest alternative approaches to problems and uncover the dispositions that direct outcomes toward good or ill.

From Adam and Eve to Joseph and Mary

PP/HW, Adam & Eve	PP/HW, Joseph & Mary
MS, Eve & Cain, Abel	MS, Mary & Jesus

Eras: Founders; Incarnation

Stories: Genesis 1:26—4:8; Matthew 1:18—2:23 and Luke 1:26—2:52.

Setting: Review Adam's and Mary's "songs" (p. 3–4) and the final featured story in chapter 5 (p. 47). The brief stories of these two famed couples impact billions of people. Their actions prove the spouses must have talked to each other, but, oddly enough, their stories note not even one conversation between just the husband and wife. We do know that God initiated conversation with each person, and how they responded defined the outcome.

To prime the pump, consider these comparisons. Eve produced life; Mary pondered life. Eve asked God no questions; Mary's question God answered. Adam took possession of every being he named; Joseph gave the name God supplied to a son who was not his. Adam and Eve looked out for themselves; Joseph and Mary looked out for Jesus. Adam worked at home; Joseph found work at three homes. Eve's son murdered; Mary's son was murdered.

As you connect the stories, find evidence for your assessment on the following:

1. advantages and disadvantages of each couple;
2. the situations God handed each couple to deal with;
3. attention and receptivity to God and to the other;
4. accuracy of communication with God and the other (read carefully);
5. inclusion of the other spouse in regard to God's directives;
6. worship of God and appreciation for each other; and
7. outcome of their decisions.

Appraise this judge's verdict on Adam and Eve *before* they ate the forbidden fruit. Adam: charged with reckless and gross negligence of both accurate disclosure of God's command and follow-through with Eve. Eve: charged with failure to exercise due diligence regarding details of God's command. The one historical artifact of their story is the drive for autonomy in the self-centered human heart. What is your verdict on Mary and Joseph?

Puzzler: Most Westerners fantasize that in the Garden of Eden all creation, living beings, man, and woman lived in perfect beauty and harmony. Furthermore, hidden in that fantasy may linger assumptions that (1) we would do right on a second chance, (2) we can still attain perfectibility despite Adam and Eve's paradigm of disobedience, and (3) we shall finally return to Eden's Paradise. What do you think about these assumptions: true or false?

Passive Isaac and Petulant Rebekah

fd, Abraham & wife for Isaac	MS, Laban's mother & Laban	PP, Abimelech & Sarah
PP, servant & Rebekah	PP, servant & Rebekah's nurse, maids	HW, Esau & Judith, Basemath
BS, Laban & Rebekah	HW, Isaac & Rebekah	fd, Isaac & Judith, Basemath
FD, Bethuel & Rebekah	MS, Rebekah & Esau, Jacob	HW, Esau & Mahalath
PP, servant & Rebekah's mother		BS, Nebaioth & Mahalath

Era: Founders

Story: Genesis 24:1—28:9, 35:8, 49:31.

Setting: Read or review the introduction to chapter 4 about fathers and daughters (p. 33). Watch family dynamics between the generations, genders, and in-laws.

No other marriage arrangement in Scripture is described in the detail found in this account. For the first marriage after Abraham and Sarah entered the covenant God offered them, Abraham required two non-negotiables for his daughter-in-law. She must come from his extended family and willingly leave her home to cling to Isaac. The latter puts the wife at a disadvantage in comparison to Genesis 2:24. The servant required of God two additional servant-like signs of divine approval. She must exhibit the physical strength to water all his camels and offer freely to do so. Oiled by luxurious gifts to Rebekah and her family, the gears of match-making ran smoothly, though her mother and brother's recommendation of a ten-day delay was declined. A good plan on papyrus, a marriage made in heaven? Maybe not.

Twenty years later God told Rebekah that the cause of her troubled pregnancy was that "two nations are in your womb … ." Yet Abraham had insisted that Isaac and his wife come from the same family. Rebekah aggressively took her interpretation of God's words into her own hands by greed, deceit, collusion, and petulance.[2] The laid-back, peace-loving Isaac remained almost clueless until his favored son cried, "Cheat!" Their family splintered.

In hindsight, we realize God defines family a different way. Yet God's severe mercy may intervene without twisting arms (hip sockets excepted).

Puzzler: The best-laid plans of men and mice often go awry. God seemed to confirm Abraham's and his servant's wishes. Rebekah filled their bill to a T. But the couple did not live happily ever after. Biblical narratives serve as examples for our instruction. What warnings and lessons can you take from this family? Without becoming too modern (we have our troubles), what changes and alternatives would you suggest to each family member, including Esau?

Boaz and Ruth: A Romance of Faith

PP, foreman & Ruth	PP, harvesters & Ruth	PP, elders & Ruth
PP/HW, Boaz & Ruth	PP/ms, Naomi & Boaz	PP, near-kinsman & Ruth
		PP, Boaz & town women

Era: Judges

Story: Ruth 2–4. See Leviticus 19:9–10, 23:22; Deuteronomy 24:19 (gleaning laws); Deuteronomy 25:5–10 (Levirate marriage); Matthew 1:3, 5 (genealogy of Jesus).

Setting: Genealogies were a source of family pride or shame. Ruth and Boaz carried tarnished characters in their family trees. A conception in drunken incest launched Ruth's national identity (see p. 35). Tamar framed her father-in-law, Judah, by playing the prostitute (review p. 24). The maternal heritage of Boaz issued from Rahab, a savvy sex trafficker and traitor who lied to officials to protect her city's enemies (see p. 69). But Matthew's genealogy of Jesus notes all of these names.

Now slowly savor the details of Boaz and Ruth moving toward marriage, a dialogue unsurpassed in Scripture. This literary jewel swells with meritorious courtesy, loyalty, faith, diligence, grace, lawfulness, generosity, respect, honor, joy, appreciation, and providential transformation in the end. Some theologians make an analogy of God and faithful believers with the Lover and Beloved of Song of Solomon. I think Boaz and Ruth fit better.

Imagine addressing the Son of Man this way. "I am [fill in your name], your servant; spread your cloak over your servant, for you are next-of-kin." Hear the ready reply, "Do not be afraid, I will do for you all that you ask." Atonement (think "at-one-ment"), "a covering" in Hebrew, signals a major theme in God's Grand Story. Forms of the word "redemption" appear 23 times in the book of Ruth. Picture God's pure delight when a wealthy, established, gentleman asked God's blessing on a young, destitute, widowed alien. Naomi's family blessed Moab, their enemies. Boaz and Ruth's blessing filled Naomi's emptiness and brought joy in Bethlehem.

Centuries later, a bright star shone overhead there and led wise men to a baby in a manger. That blessing keeps spreading around the world. Abraham still smiles at the fulfillment of the covenant which welcomed the likes of Ruth and Boaz.

Puzzler: This is the only Old Testament story of a marriage chiefly based upon the faith-filled characters of the bride and groom. Silence about physical beauty, bridal price, political advantage, steamy eroticism, and ethnic solidarity keeps the main thing the main thing. Boaz's opening words to the reapers, "The LORD be with you," recalibrate the path to come. When did an event you know of occur chiefly through faith in God's active presence?

From Ahab and Jezebel to Jehoiada and Jehoshebeath: Bad Blood

HW, King Ahab & Queen Jezebel in Israel	FD, Ahab & Athaliah
HW, Jehoram (son of King Jehoshaphat in Judah) & Athaliah	FD, Jehoram & Jehoshebeath
MS, Athaliah & Ahaziah	BS, Ahaziah & Jehoshebeath (grandfathers: paternal Jehoshaphat, maternal Ahab)
ms, Grandmother Athaliah & line of David, Joash (son of Ahaziah)	HW, Jehoiada & Jehoshebeath
ms, Aunt Jehoshebeath & Joash	PP, Elijah & Jezebel
PP, Joash & nurse	

Era: Kingdom, divided into Judah in the south, ruled by the line of David; and Israel in the north, ruled by the line of Ahab, son of Omri. Israel regularly fell into Baal worship.

Story: 1 Kings 16:29—17:6, 18:1—20:22, and 22 (Ahab and Jezebel); 2 Chronicles 21–24 (preferred) or 2 Kings 8:16—12:21 (Jehoiada and Jehoshebeath). Spellings of names vary.

Setting: Baal (sun god) and Asherah (moon goddess) exalted fertility through orgiastic rituals with temple prostitutes of both sexes. Canaanite farmers prayed for fertile soil while Hebrew shepherds prayed for reproducing animals. Ritual prostitution presented a powerful temptation and competed against the invisible LORD of covenant fidelity.

Jehoshaphat, Judah's king in the line of David, sought the Word of the LORD during his reign. When Israel's King Ahab married Queen Jezebel from Sidon, Baal worship infiltrated Israel. When their daughter, Athaliah, married Jehoram, Crown Prince of Judah, he followed her and her mother into Baal worship. Their son, Ahaziah, reigned in Judah briefly as a puppet of his mother. Upon his murder, Athaliah seized the throne of Judah to become the only woman ruler in Hebrew history. She attempted to wipe out the line of David, including her own grandsons.

Jesus commented on the bloody end of this story.[3] Careful readers learn three lessons here. First, choice of spouse matters now and forever. Second, God remembers courage with kindness even if things go badly. Third, good kings can have sons that are bad kings, like Jehoshaphat and his son Jehoram. Bad kings can have faithful offspring and in-laws, like Jehoram and his daughter Jehoshebeath, married to the priest Jehoiada.

Puzzler: Both weeping Jeremiah and exiled Ezekiel contested the old proverb, "The parents have eaten sour grapes, and the children's teeth are set on edge." Jeremiah 31:27–30 and Ezekiel 18 record their sober conclusions. Although parents and spouses can nurture, neglect, or confuse faith formation, each of us bears responsibility for our faith. That *may* cause discontinuity between generations. What words of wisdom and hope might apply in your family tree?

The Seventy, the Apostles, and Traveling Wives: Commissioned Couples

HW, among the Seventy	HW, Jesus's brothers, apostles & wives

Eras: Incarnation (the Seventy); Church (various apostles)

Story: The Seventy (or 72): Luke 10:1–20. Instructions to traveling disciples: Matthew 10:1, 9–14, Mark 6:7–13, Luke 9:1–6. Church era: 1 Corinthians 9:1–18 *note verses 5–6.*

Setting: In the first century CE, the infrastructure for travel exceeded and excelled that of any previous time because Rome ruled an extensive territory surrounding the Mediterranean Sea. Commerce including the slave trade, warfare, diplomacy, and state-building efforts accounted for the vast majority of travelers. Extensive Roman roads of stone resisted flooding and were wide enough for six soldiers marching side by side. Segments and some milestones still exist. Guards kept watch on roads near cities. On secondary gravel roads and dirt paths, travelers carrying their money and goods might encounter thieves, robbers, wild animals, and hazardous weather. Accommodations at numerous inns added expenses. Sea travel was preferred for both shorter shoreline stops and more distant destinations across the Mediterranean, but shipwreck and storms made voyages impossible for part of the year and arrival times uncertain.

In Palestine, boating across the Sea of Galilee usually made better time than walking around the sea. The shallow Jordan River was unsuitable for boats. Land travelers walked in groups for safety and used pack animals to carry goods. The Seventy probably did not take children on these dangerous and tiring mission journeys. Extended family could care for them.

Among Jesus's devoted disciples, Luke named married and unmarried women who traveled with him and provided for his ministry from their own funds.[4] The half-brother of Jesus, James, headed the church in Jerusalem. His other brothers Joseph, Judas, and Simon along with Cephas/Peter and other apostles traveled *with their wives* to spread the Gospel. Paul noted this in his letter to Corinth. Paul's letters to the Corinthians were written before the Gospels. By the time the Gospels were written, this practice did not need to be mentioned because it was assumed. Assuredly the Seventy Jesus sent out on mission included spouses visiting relatives and their neighboring villages.

Puzzler: Imagine this scenario: the apostle Bartholomew and his wife, Sarah, visit her cousin Mark in Cana, Galilee. At dinner, Bart reclines at table with Mark and his two sons while Sarah helps the women serve the food. Before everyone spreads sleeping mats on the roof, they chat under the stars in the cool night breeze. The topic focuses on the rapid church growth in Jerusalem. How might spouses separately and together enhance introducing the Gospel?

Aquila and Priscilla: Tentmaking Teachers

HW, Aquila & Priscilla	PP, Apollos & Priscilla
PP, Paul & Priscilla	PP, church at home of Priscilla & Aquila

Era: Church

Story: Acts 18–19; Romans 16:3–5; 1 Corinthians 16:19; 2 Timothy 4:19.

Setting: See the previous story for a description of first-century travel in the Roman Empire. Rome encouraged religious festivals and games that attracted thousands. For such events, tents provided for selling wares and for temporary housing. In quality, tents ran the spectrum from small shelters to luxurious residences. Sought-out religious intellectuals, sophists, sages, and wise men also traveled widely. The Jews had agitated several times for more privileges, and records show controversies about "Crestus," perhaps referring to Christ. Rome classified Christianity as a cult within Judaism early in the Church's history, and officials acted to squelch public conflicts. Such disturbances led to expulsions of Jews in 139 BCE, 19 CE, and around 50 CE when Gallio was proconsul and Claudius was emperor (41–54 CE).

Acts records several such disturbances caused by the preaching of Christ by Paul and other apostles. In this context, Priscilla and Aquila had to leave Italy and took their tentmaking business first to Corinth, where they met Paul, and finally to Ephesus. Paul used his extensive time working with them to teach intensely. He had confidence that these close friends were prepared to lead the church and to teach Apollos thoroughly about faith in Christ (see p. 99). Ephesus became a center for Christianity, which spread from there throughout the region. Atypically, Priscilla is often mentioned first, indicating her predominance. A practice today derived from this story helps pioneering ministries get off the ground. A "tentmaker" works bi-vocationally in ministry with financial support from other employment.

Couples like Mary with Joseph, Cleopas with his wife, the traveling apostles with their wives, and Priscilla with Aquila give us examples of God's original intentions for marriage as men and women together cultivated and tended God's "garden."[5] They offered united energy, even risking their goods and lives, to serve Jesus and the Church. Their mutual labor as image-bearing icons pointed the world to the Triune God.

Puzzler: In review, notice that God's Grand Story has brought us a long way from Adam and Eve, Isaac and Rebekah, Boaz and Ruth, Ahab and Jezebel, and Ahasuerus and Esther. Even though culture and time create a distance, identify traits and actions that served these couples well or damaged their marriages. For good or ill, which couples thus far in this small book linger in your memory? Why might that be?

Supplemental Stories

Whether one is single or married, marriage, as the apostle Paul says, remains "a great mystery" and a metaphor for Christ and the Church.[6] This covenant offers the locus for the focus of love learned in daily life together. Appraise these marriages by using Paul's metaphor.

Sons of God and Daughters of Men
Era: Founders. Story: Genesis 2:23, 6:1–8.
Man's initial exclamation *can* suggest that men are sons of God (come from God) while women are daughters of men (come from men).[7] See what God did about it.

Job and Wife
Eras: Founders (oral tradition), Kingdom (wisdom literature). Story: Job 1:1—2:10, 42:10–17.
The pain of those who watch loved ones go through devastating losses can cut with a sharp edge. Think twice before passing judgment on Job's wife for her famous one-liner.

Jacob and Leah (Zilpah), Rachel (Bilhah)
Era: Founders. Story: Genesis 29–31.
Men compete with each other, but these sisters played hardball, too. They competed for Jacob while he competed with Laban to keep all his hungry mouths filled.

Hosea and Gomer
Era: Kingdom. Story: Hosea 1–3.
Love betrayed bursts open emotions so raw that sanity buckles. Hosea wades through the depths to reveal a higher order of transcending love meant to restore, reconcile, and reunite.

Pontius Pilate and [Claudia Procula]
Era: Incarnation. Matthew 27:11–26.
Had Pilate known that millions worldwide stand weekly to affirm the Creed, "[Jesus] was crucified under Pontius Pilate," he might have listened to his wife. Why didn't he?

Ananias and Sapphira
Era: Church. Story: Acts 5:1–11.
People resist fear-motivated religion. But perhaps we actually need to squirm a bit when we pray, "to you all hearts are open, all desires known, and from you no secrets are hid."[8]

8

Sexual Encounters: Liaisons outside Marriage

Scene 1: God's Grand Story begins with wisdom and delight.[1] Scripture declares from the outset that God's purpose for the male and female of humankind included sexual encounters. The Creator told the man and the woman to be fruitful and multiply. *Together* they were to reflect the plurality and unity of God to their offspring and the wider creation. And everything God made was very good.

Scene 2: When God brought the woman, later named Eve, to the man, later named Adam, he let out an excited cry of pleasure (review p. 3). The man never let on, but this match-up was not his idea. *God* saw that it was not good for the man to be alone. Adam omitted two details in his rendition of Eve's origins: God formed Eve; Adam was asleep. Eve learned only two half-truths from Adam: her source was Adam's body, period, and her identity came from Adam, period. Being self-aware and God-aware, he had to have known better. Therefore, he reneged on two obligations incumbent upon him: acknowledging the Creator's forming hand and thanking God. That left Eve in the dark and beholden to Adam.

Scene 3 and beyond: Not being an arm-twister, God watched Adam and Eve bumble along their own self-centered courses. Not taken by surprise, God knew that the course of true love brings together two self-centered people, even when "a man leaves his father and his mother and clings to his wife, and they become one flesh."[2] The Bible never wavers from affirming this plan but reports counterexamples. Many couples have decided not to follow that route and consented to fornication or adultery.[3] This chapter features some of their stories.

The reasons for taking one of these paths usually boils down to pride or the other side of this counterfeit coin, fear. Seven (the "complete" number) prime promoters of pride appear here in alphabetical order: pleasure, popularity, possessions, power, privilege, prosperity, and protection. "Fear not" comes scores of times from God's mouth. Jesus and his beloved disciple assure us, "There is no fear in love, but perfect love casts out fear."[4] No two human lovers reach perfect love, but our hearts can find *shalom* in God's love.

The Trinity brings us love, goodness itself. Evil has no substance of its own but only diminishes goodness by impairing it, messing it up, misrepresenting it, and taking it in a wrong way. Evil corrupts good, but God exposes the deceits of evil and defeats them with truth. That pattern intensifies and diversifies in the unfolding plot of God's Grand Story. In the following narratives, watch pride, its seven cousins above, and fear do their work.

Pharaoh, Abimelech, and Sarai/Sarah: Saving Her Husband's Skin

bs/HW, Abram & Sarai	HW, Abraham & Sarah
hw, Pharaoh & Sarai	PP, Abimelech & Sarah

Era: Founders

Story: Genesis 12:10–20 (Pharaoh episode); Genesis 20 (Abimelech episode).

Setting: Nomads and their animals co-existed with settled crop growers. Their lives and organization differed. Nomadic groups comprised a close-knit family or clan headed by a patriarchal figure, and were not threatening unless they became large and competed for the limited water supply. Here today, gone before long. Larger and more diverse agricultural communities throughout Egypt and the smaller area of Gerar required more complex rules and regulations about family bonds and sexual behavior. Whether patriarch, pharaoh, or king, these holders of power considered themselves a privileged class entitled to satisfying their sexual desires. However, they also had learned that adultery and fornication could cause social and health problems that were worth avoiding.

A merciful God watching the mistakes we make allows and expects us to learn from these failures and gives us repeated chances to improve. But the recalcitrant lure of sex appeal combined with fear of loss creates a charged situation. Take One: Right after Abram obeyed God's call to move to a new land, this problem put in an appearance. Abram had been raised in the fertile valleys of the Tigris and Euphrates Rivers, but famine recurred in the hill country to which God called him. When the famine became severe, he set off to the nearest fertile river, the Nile. To protect himself, he told a white lie. While it did not turn out well, it did turn out profitably. Take Two: After God changed Abram's and Sarai's names to Abraham and Sarah, the same situation occurred, except there was no famine this time. Sarah colluded in the white lie. Abimelech's land was closer than Egypt. Spurred on by God's intervention, he dealt with Abraham so that they could co-exist. Explanation, confession, restitution, and prayer brought reconciliation. It turned out quite profitably for Abraham, too. Sad to say, right after God renewed the covenant with Isaac, he tried his dad's trick in Genesis 26 but with an outright falsehood. But it did *not* turn out profitable. It didn't happen again. When it comes to lust, we are slow learners.

Puzzler: Isn't it ironic that the good guys taking a moral stance had to reprimand God's chosen Abraham for his dishonesty? They had standards ready and in place. They had learned something Abraham had not. Trace God's action in the two Abrahamic stories and Isaac's fiasco. If God could give Abraham a specific promise, God could also have told him directly not to fudge about Sarah. What was God trying to accomplish? What do you think of God's methods?

The Israelite Spies and Rahab: Redemption and Rehabilitation

NM, spies & Rahab, women of the house	BS, Rahab's brothers & Rahab
FD, Rahab's father & Rahab	PP, Joshua & Rahab

Era(s): Transition from Exodus to Judges

Story: Joshua 2–6. See also Matthew 1:5; Hebrews 11:31; James 2:25.

Setting: The Israelites approached the Promised Land from the Jordan River's east side. Jericho lay five miles west of the Jordan near the Dead Sea, and Gilgal lay northeast of Jericho. Inside walled cities, one side or portion of a house could be the wall itself. Partitioned rooms within deep, hollow walls also provided living space. Inns, located strategically near the gates, accommodated travelers. Innkeepers could see approaching strangers through windows that looked out of the city. Even today some inns unofficially offer an amenity of paid bed partners. A male grad school religion professor quipped that these encounters are "as routine as bowel movements and as satisfying as eating watermelon." Hmm, ask Judah.

Since Rahab had no husband or children, running such an inn gave her a livelihood and shelter. Its high window facing outward takes a central role in this well-known spy story. Travelers gathering here were shaking in their sandals about the powerful God who had parted the Red Sea and conquered nearby cities for the Israelites. When two of them checked in for her hospitality, Rahab took a traitorous risk fueled by faith in *their* God. Together they pledged to an escape plan for her and her family. Her intrigue brought on an even more comprehensive and traumatic transition than Ruth's would be years later.

Symbolically and geographically, the Israelites crossing the Jordan River marked their pivotal transition with five changes: (1) trust passed to Joshua after Moses's death; (2) attitudes changed from fear to confidence; (3) wandering ended as they set foot in the Promised Land; (4) devotion was rekindled with circumcision and celebration of the Passover; and (5) the manna ceased, requiring them to labor for the fruit and grain of the land. Ground-shaking! Preparation for this pivotal point from slavery to freedom took 40 years. God is still patient.

Moving to the next degree of love for self and God necessitates transitions, as the examples in chapter 2 recall. God always goes before pilgrims, both preparing the way and maintaining continuity.

Puzzler: A reader might raise this question about Rahab's moral character: Did she just need an escape or was her faith truly bonded to Israel's God? Jesus recommended judging the tree by its fruit.[5] From the fruit of this one-time prostitute came Boaz, the most honorable gentleman in the Bible apart from Jesus. This heritage granted him discernment of faith in another despised foreign woman, and he welcomed her. What other factors apply to your take on Rahab?

Hophni, Phinehas, and Women at the Tent of Meeting: Scandal at Shiloh

HW, Elkanah & Hannah	MS, Hannah & Samuel	NM, Hophni, Phinehas & servers
PP, Eli & Hannah		MS, wife of Phinehas & Ichabod

Era: Judges

Story: 1 Samuel 2:12—4:22. Review the era of Judges (p. 13).

Setting: Samuel's work maintained the continuity of God's covenant with Israel during the precarious transition from leadership by tribal judges to national kings. The tent of meeting at Shiloh served as a central place of worship in Israel. The innermost part of the tent housed the Ark of the Covenant, a gold-covered chest holding the tables of the Law and other sacred objects. The "Mercy Seat" lay under the touching tips of raised wings of two cherubim carved on either side of the Ark's cover. Priests wore a vest called an ephod, kept the incense burning (symbolizing instruction and prayer), and supervised the sacrifices offered. People brought sacrifices to the tent for reconciliation, thanksgiving, and confirmation of loyalty to the God of the covenant, often accompanied by vows. The fat of the sacrifice was first reserved for God. Then Priests received a portion of the meat a fork could hold before the worshipers enjoyed the remainder of the sacrifice. Three times a year, families gathered to celebrate God's deliverance from Pharaoh and provision during their wilderness wandering. The priests invoked the LORD's blessing on the cycle of planting, first fruits, and harvest. During these festivities, an inebriated worshiper might enter the tent. Abuse of worship was tantamount to treason.

Tracing the paths of Hophni and Phinehas demonstrates three violations of the covenant. First, they greedily demanded more than their share of the sacrifices, a lingering practice that made Eli literally obese. Second, their adulterous sexual encounters with women who cleaned the kitchen at sacrifices mimicked regional fertility religions. Third, they audaciously used the Ark as a fetish or good luck charm in battle, crossing the limit of God's patience. Disrespect for the sacred came to a screeching halt for three generations of Eli's family.

But God gave Samuel eyes to see these infractions and ears to hear God's voice breaking through the din. Never fear that God has run out of rescue plans.

Puzzler: In our modern cause-and-effect world, we doubt that a young, impressionable boy could escape the corrupting influence of Eli's sons, who refused to terminate their wicked practices. Yet Samuel learned, respected, and taught the people the Commandments (review p. 14). What do you believe about God speaking directly to a person? Does God still do that today? How might it happen?

David and Bathsheba: Power Corrupted

HW, Uriah & Bathsheba	PP, Nathan & Bathsheba	MS, Bathsheba & unnamed son
NM/HW, David & Bathsheba		MS, Bathsheba & Solomon

Era: Kingdom

Story: 2 Samuel 11–12; Psalm 51; Matthew 1:6 (note the name omitted in this verse). See also the stories of Bathsheba (p. 45) and Tamar (p. 53).

Setting: In the ancient world, people revered their kings like saviors. Kings often had won wars that protected and enriched their subjects. In spring, after crops had been planted, it was time to go out and take more land to increase the next year's yield. Kings desired to expand and consolidate the people and land they ruled. They also could take from the conquered what they thought they could get away with, including women and goods. The word of these revered men was law, and they held the power of life and death in their hands. Many rulers aspired to being viewed as deities or at least as the mouths of the gods of the land.

Samuel had both given warnings and set principles for the monarchy. In Israel, the king was to live *under*, not *over*, the conditions of the covenant with the LORD God. Saul had failed, but David reached the zenith of his success in favor with God and people. Once when spring approached, he decided to take a break because Joab could handle the war season. Then David failed by breaking several of the Ten Commandments. Most of his contemporary chieftains and kings would not have condemned him for what he did in his free time. But Nathan no doubt lost sleep over how to address the problem. God gave him the words. Providentially, David trusted Nathan's loyalty as a friend, respected his office as a prophet, and confessed to the LORD.

Let's not condemn David until we have searched our own imaginings about people who have stood in the way of what we desired. Then daydream about claiming an exception to normal consequences and having the power to do what we want. At that point, everyone, kings and peons, leaves reality behind. Despite our best scientific, economic, and political predictions, human beings have a poor record on foreseeing the future.

God forgave David. The next featured story traces the undreamed-of consequences for David, his children, Bathsheba, his concubines, his top leaders, his enemies, and the nation.

Puzzler: Israelites and Hittites lived in the same territory and intermarried against God's will. Abraham bought his burial cave from a Hittite. The freed Israelites took Hittite cities and forced many into slave labor. But Uriah the Hittite rose to be a loyal and mighty warrior for David.[6] Later Solomon sold horses to Hittites and brought their women into his huge harem. What inner conflicts might this have raised for the bather, widow, and Queen Mother Bathsheba?

Absalom and David's Ten Concubines: Power Usurped

BS, Absalom & Tamar	PP, David & wise woman	NM, Absalom & concubines
bs/NM, Amnon & Tamar	FD, Absalom & Tamar (14:27)	PP, Jonathan, Ahimaaz & servant-girl
FD, David & Tamar	NM, David & concubines	HW, couple with well
PP, Joab & wise woman	PP, Ahithophel & concubines	PP, Absalom's men & wife

Era: Kingdom

Story: 2 Samuel 13:20—18:33, particularly 15:16, 16:21–23, 20:3. Backstory: 12:7–15.

Setting: Just as men contrived hierarchies, they also formed hierarchies for the women of the palace(s). If you read the story of Rizpah (see p. 44), you learned that concubines might serve the sexual desires of a wealthy man, but they had none of the legal privileges of a wife. They may have been taken as loot in war or purchased from another owner. Usually their duties focused on labor in their owner's house. Lower yet were women who worked in the fields. The poor like Ruth gleaned what was left behind. You may recall from the story of Esther that it was an honor to ride a horse the king had ridden or to wear one of his robes. But sleeping with his concubine(s) signaled sedition against him and invited vengeance from any owner.

As David's family unravels, the author's account drives home the truth that sin is never "private." Individualistic societies largely deny this fact by drawing a wall between private and public life. The effects of David's sin soon spread in an ever-widening circle to his partner, their baby, his military commander Joab, his army's defeat, his partner's husband Uriah, the prophet Nathan, his household servants, his sons, the wise woman of Tekoa, his daughter and granddaughter (both named Tamar), his nation, their enemy nations, his concubines, his advisors, and the citizenry. Adultery finally threatened his throne. The princes figured that if Dad could get away with exploiting a woman and murder, so could they. They took his sin to crueler levels. And what of the fate of the ten concubines? David ascertained that none of them had produced a tainted grandson by Absalom (whew!) and ignored them sexually ever after. Neither did his wives receive much attention from the declining king. But there is good news.

God used all this evil to spare Israel two potential heirs to the throne, the deplorable Amnon and Absalom. By God's grace, the imperfect Solomon made a far better king.

Puzzler: David's office of king certainly had a more profound effect than that of an average citizen. However, his example granted permission. Even though Nathan's story convicted the moral character of David, it certainly did not for others. In a time of conflicted sexual relations in individual, community, workplace, and national arenas, how relevant is this story today? What ideas and actions might deter exploitation and related violence?

Lawyers and the Adulterous Woman: Justice with Mercy

PP/NM?, lawyers & the woman	PP, Jesus & the woman

Era: Incarnation

Story: John 7:53—8:11. For what the Law said about sex outside marriage, see the situations given in Exodus 22:16, Leviticus 19:20–22, 20:10, and Deuteronomy 22:13–30.

Setting: The system of punishments and fines in the well-known Code of Hammurabi in Babylon (18th century BCE) was based on the social classes of the offender and the offended. The value accorded to women was at most roughly equal to that accorded to milking cows. Several centuries later, Moses's sensitivity to the poor came through his people's heritage of oppression in slavery. Laws protected Israel's slaves and gave them hope for freedom. Slavery also existed in the Roman world of Jesus's lifetime, many centuries after Moses. The Jewish people, because they hoped for a Messiah, had high respect for the covenant of marriage with its careful pre-nuptial negotiations between the family of bride and groom, high expectations of fidelity, and records of lineage. A betrothal agreement did not allow for sexual intercourse, but the couple's commitment could be severed only by divorce.

This story relates a scathing denouncement of the religious leaders. They could have secluded the woman in question during the proceedings. Instead, they not only framed her but also shamed her with public humiliation. Jesus refused to speak to them at first. The Word bent to write words in the dust. Then in one sentence his pronouncement pilloried publicly their hypocritical double standard and flagrant misuse of the Law. He stooped again to write on the ground. Imagine the LORD of heaven bowed down before this framed and shamed woman. When he looked up again, the woman's accusers had abandoned her, but not Jesus. He upheld the Law, brought justice, exercised mercy, and freed the captive by his spoken and written words.

Salvation found this woman directly east of Jerusalem on the Mount of Olives. At this site, Jesus prepared his disciples for future perils, pronounced sorrowfully the destruction of the Temple, obtained a colt for his Triumphal Entry into Jerusalem, warned Peter of his denials to come, prayed in the Garden of Gethsemane at its base, and finally ascended into heaven. Here Satan's defeat was assured. It is holy ground from the dust to the clouds.

Puzzler: I am not surprised that this story had a hard time finding a slot to enter the Gospels.[7] It still makes men and women squirm, especially in this time of heightened awareness of sexual abuse by clergy. Much rides on what Jesus wrote on the ground (the only reference to his writing), which we will never know. Whatever he wrote neither misrepresented the truth nor contradicted the Law. How satisfied are you with the ending?

Supplemental Stories

The absence of a covenant in a sexual partnership or marriage is rarely noted in our culture's storytelling. You can readily ascertain this by citing movies that include assiduous respect *before* a sexual encounter. Foreplay frequently trumps forethought. Notice the intent to record the role of pride and its seven cousins (review p. 67) in these true cautionary tales.

Shechem and Dinah
Era: Founders. Story: Genesis 34.
Religion can be a weapon. Contrast the honor of Shechem and of Judah's sons. Read between the lines to consider why one party's desires and words never surface.

Amnon and Tamar
Era: Kingdom. Story: 2 Samuel 13, Leviticus 20:17.
Tamar leaves no doubt about her wishes. Lust can turn on a dime to betrayal and utter contempt! Contrast the character of this male predator with the man in the previous story.

Zimri and Cozbi
Era: Exodus. Story: Numbers 25.
This story grates on the nerves of our current commitment to inclusivity. However, it is naïve to think objects of worship make little difference in sexual partnerships. Be warned.

Belshazzar and Concubines
Era: Exile. Story: Daniel 5.
It's party time, folks! Wealth provides lavish dining and free drinks for even the lowly concubines. But God calls this parade of pride a charade and draws the curtains on it.

Reforms of Ezra and Nehemiah
Era: Exile. Story: Ezra 9:1—10:44; Nehemiah 13:23–31.
These reformers recognized that marriages would form the foundation and shape the future of the Jewish remnant returning home after seventy years in Babylonian exile.

Corinthian Man and Stepmother
Era: Church. Story: 1 Corinthians 5.
Are you surprised that nuggets from this unequivocal story show up in the celebration of Holy Communion? Thanks be to God, our Paschal lamb has been slain to forgive the repentant.

Cupid's Confessions

What influences the sexual partnerships we enter? The two chapters in this part about sexual liaisons show us that Cupid may have arrows, but most often it is parents, siblings, peers, economic and political factors, religious and ethnic loyalties, social standing, national identities, and even God that draw the bow. Even if it is drawn well, Cupid's arrows frequently fail to yield bliss. Is it really much different today? From infancy through adulthood, we store memories, particularly of the family dynamics at home, and glean input from them for decisions about sexual behavior. Seeing interactions of other couples and families, influences of friends, and actions based on faith, plus hearing stories told at home, churches, schools, and media add to our repertoire of approaches to sexual intimacy. The communities in which we participate and the laws and mores they endorse finally have an important say in these matters.

The Bible neither labors nor hides these factors from the perceptive reader. Effective examples tend to exude pungent or perfumed aromas that stick in our minds and move our emotions. They serve the purposes of instruction, not Cupid's capers. They offer us no magic formulas that guarantee blissful sexual intimacy, let alone fertility. Nor does God show signs and wonders to confirm our choices. Such superstition only deflects from our responsibility to exercise wisdom in these crucial decisions. "Therefore marriage is not to be entered into unadvisedly or lightly, but reverently, deliberately, and in accordance with the purposes for which it was instituted by God."[1] The Almighty promises to answer prayers for wisdom.[2]

Parallels between marriage and spiritual life figure prominently in biblical teaching. It leaves no doubt about how God views infidelity and fidelity outside and during marriage. When the Israelites broke the covenant, God, their figurative husband, called it "whoredom" and the men and women participating "adulteresses."[3] Israel's frequent falls into the sexual rites of Baal worship illustrate yielding to counterfeit spirituality. God woos them back.

A pastor preparing a couple for marriage may ask them to articulate the difference between a marriage contract and a covenant, and present the model of the interaction of Father, Holy Spirit, and Son. A contract has start and end dates, with stipulated actions for each party; covenantal promises forge a love-based way of life bounded only by death. Marriages founded in wisdom and trustworthy character reflect the image of God. HE, SHE, and THREE (the Trinity) become WE, radiating self-giving love. Welcome *shalom.*

A home is not a cozy space for insulated intimacy, but rather life at home conditions and predicts how we will live outside the home, as we shall see in the next part of this book.

PART IV

PEERS IN THE PLOT: COMPASSIONATE AND COMBUSTIBLE COMBINATIONS

When I was compiling the stories for this project, packages of colored 3" × 5" cards suited for notes on relationships between the genders: yellow for fathers and daughters, green for mothers and sons, orange for brothers and sisters, red for sexual liaisons, and blue for peers in the plot. To my surprise, the blue cards had to be replenished more than once. Accounts of men and women connected neither by blood nor by sexual involvement skyrocket in the New Testament. Just Jesus and Paul account for over 50 examples of women peers. I shouldn't have been surprised, but the Church historically has focused more teaching on family and marriage than on peers and colleagues in a co-ed world. Furthermore, the centuries-old tradition of all male clergy and gender-segregated service gave clergy little experience with female colleagues.

Though long underestimated, peers in the plot bring us intriguing stories in diverse settings. Paging through chapters 1–3 yields a sampling of influential peers. The man and woman were created primarily as co-workers (peers in God's image) to care for God's creation. Thomas confirmed Mary Magdalene's report of the risen Jesus and proclaimed him Lord and God. Two lowly midwives defied Pharaoh to save Moses who freed the Hebrew slaves. Queen Esther's courageous confrontation of wicked Haman elevated her eminence before the king. His response upended laws making wives subservient to their husbands. King Josiah's reforms under the prophet Huldah staved off calamity to his nation. To introduce the Messiah, Jesus and the woman at the well in Sychar together breached walls of historic antagonism between Israel and Samaria. More breached walls of status, religion, ethnicity, and nationality appear in the next three chapters from the Hebrew Bible, the Gospels, and the early church.

Exclusive bonds between spouses and among family members play a vital role in preparing the next generation to move out of the home into the wider world as agents of trust, peace, and productivity. When Jesus taught that all believers are made children of God, he used familial terms within the Holy Trinity as a model. From the Resurrection on (see p. 110), God has placed sisters and brothers in Christ where they fulfill Jesus's Great Commission. Together they have gone into all the world to preach, teach, and live the Gospel in covenantal accord.

God's Grand Story continually moves forward to restore to creation and humanity our true selves and purpose. Believers become living stones of a spiritual house that proclaims God's mighty acts to bring people out of darkness into marvelous light.[1]

9

Old Testament Peers: Compassion and Courage

Old Testament nomadic families, clans, and tribes established traditions to secure the current and ongoing line of generations. Fathers negotiated carefully to arrange marriages for their sons and daughters that would be as advantageous as their means could attain. Since men were considered more important than women as laborers and protectors, they stayed within the clan after marriage. Normally a young woman who did not marry within the clan could be exported to join her husband's family (see p. 43). In the Kingdom era, these negotiations intensified to strengthen political alliances with other nations. Women and men had little contact or conversation with each other outside the home. All these safeguards for continuity, birth, and marriage, followed by the next generation of births and marriages, looked good on papyrus.

So how could men and women associate as peers without blood ties or sexual liaisons? Alas, war, famine, disease, death, disabilities, and all the varieties of interpersonal conflict disrupted traditions. One has to search diligently for single men and women in the Old Testament. After being expelled by Abraham and Sarah, Hagar acted as a single parent and negotiated Ishmael's marriage. The midwives Shiphrah and Puah were single when they intervened with baby Moses, but later God gave them their own families. After being disgraced, Dinah and Absalom's sister Tamar endured childless life in their brothers' homes. Abishag, the beautiful Shunammite, remained a virgin while she kept the elderly David warm in bed. The deposed Queen Vashti was probably sustained by state funds, and some historians think she may have been reinstated later. Wealthy men kept concubines as laborers. Other husbandless women earned money as temple/tent prostitutes or inn hostesses like Rahab, who later married. Other possibly single women were sought for their insights and visions at a price, but sorceresses, mediums, and wizards were supposed to be outlawed in Israel. The rare single men appear in the Exile era: eunuchs who served kings such as those listed in the book of Esther and, by conjecture, the war captives, Daniel and his three friends, Shadrach, Meshach, and Abednego. They served in high offices, but the royalty had most likely made it impossible for them to produce children who might become rivals for the throne.

The heritage of slavery and Moses's experience as a fugitive gave Israel sensitivity to the plight of people assailed by injustice, oppression, and tragedy. The Old Testament Law, prophets, and wisdom writers repeatedly urged provision for the needs of the widow, orphan, and alien. There would be dire consequences for nations that ignored these weighty matters in the eyes of the all-seeing LORD. Obedience required aid through compassionate peers.

Moses and the Five Daughters of Zelophehad: Doing What Is Right

FD, Zelophehad & Mahlah, Noah, Hoglah, Milcah, Tirzah	PP, Moses & 5 daughters of the late Zelophehad

Era: Exodus

Story: Four lists name the five daughters: Numbers 26:33 (census), 27:1–11 (nearest of kin specified), 36:5–12 (tribal land allotment retained); and Joshua 17:3 (tribal borders). In a later genealogical list, 1 Chronicles 7:15 mentions them but without their names.

Setting: Wealth in an agrarian society is measured by the amount of land used legally. Israelite spies had taken into account Canaan's terrain and viable areas for pasture and crop cultivation. Accordingly, Moses assigned to each tribe a region of land in proportion to its population. Once land was allotted, it was never to be traded or passed among the tribes, or its borders moved. Thus, each tribe would have equal wealth passed from son to grandson for perpetuity. The premise was that all land belonged to God, so the people were to act as just stewards as God had intended from the beginning. To remind the people of the proper owner, Moses instituted a sabbath for the land every seven years, when they should not till, plant, prune, or reap but eat only what the land produced naturally. But God and Moses also understood the realities of greed and need and sloth. In the 50th year after seven sabbath years came the Year of Jubilee, when all land reverted to the originally assigned tribal allotment. If a man had to sell use of part or all of his land to pay debts he had incurred, he knew that the land would return to his family. The price of land decreased annually as the Year of Jubilee approached. Any man with a normal life span could look forward to at least one Year of Jubilee.

But what would happen to a man's name and attached land if he had no son? Enter the five brotherless and fatherless daughters after Zelophehad's death. He must have told them about being descendants of the great Israelite Joseph and his Egyptian son Manasseh. His parents had streaked blood on the doorposts of the house before their hasty Passover meal, and God had delivered them from slavery. But they had doubted that Israel could take the Promised Land and had died in the wilderness. Zelophehad did not want to lose the land that would keep his name alive forever. They must keep appealing to the judges until they reached Moses himself.

Puzzler: It is quite a coup that these five women's names are recorded three times in the Torah (Genesis through Deuteronomy) and once in Joshua. Their case set two historic legal precedents. The influence of Jethro, Moses's father-in-law, whose total offspring were seven girls, may have won the day. Economic justice is far more complex today. What injustice troubles you enough to limit your options willingly in order to rectify the situation?

Joshua and Rahab: Disciplined Trust

NM/PP, two spies & Rahab	PP, Joshua & Rahab
PP, King of Jericho & Rahab	PP, two spies & women at Rahab's inn

Era: Exodus

Story: Joshua 2, 6 *note verses 22–25*. Backstories: Exodus 2:15–22 and 18 (Jethro/Reuel); Numbers 13–14 (Joshua's spying); Joshua 24 *note verse 15* (Joshua's legacy). See also Hebrews 11:31.

Setting: See the story of the Israelite spies and Rahab (p. 69) for the immediate background. During the Israelites' slavery in Egypt, military skills and equipment improved, but they had little access to daggers and swords, chariots, animals trained for battle, and skillfully crafted bows and arrows. Previously fought as hand-to-hand combat, battles were now fought at distances, using the tops of the walls that now surrounded cities. Jericho's strategic location near the Jordan River and Dead Sea made it the gateway to the land west of the Jordan where Abraham's nomadic family had roamed with their livestock. Stories of his family lived on by being passed down for centuries through the generations. People today may doubt the accuracy of oral tradition because we make written records, but illiterate people retain information by memorization, and they can carefully preserve stories word for word from a young age. Even aged patriarchs could retain these stories after the onset of memory loss.

Moses's education in Pharaoh's palace taught him literacy, history, law, warfare and diplomacy, religion, record keeping, trade and commerce, and government. Jethro/Reuel taught Moses survival in the wilderness and the art of delegation to handle disputes. His hierarchy of trustworthy judges raised up many God-honoring leaders. First among them, young Joshua watched Moses daily to learn leadership skills firsthand. Moses chose him as one of twelve spies to assess the Promised Land. Forty years later, Joshua commissioned two men to spy out Jericho. The outcome of this story was the reward of years of trust-building mentors who could perceive Rahab's faith. They negotiated a deal, confident that Joshua would honor it, and he did.

These peers trusted each other and shared Joshua's decision to serve the LORD. Joshua, the spies, and Rahab made a threefold cord not quickly broken.[1] God's cord is blood red.

Puzzler: The striking thing about this story is Rahab's readiness to receive the two Hebrew spies in peace and the spies' readiness to protect her and her family. They were lined up as enemies. Yet God bonded the three to give us an example of Abraham's descendants blessing outsiders as the covenant stipulated. How do you come to trust another person, and what do you do to teach your children to discern trustworthiness in others?

King Solomon and the Queen of Sheba: The Works of Wisdom

PP, Solomon & 2 prostitutes	PP, Solomon & Queen of Sheba
MS, 2 prostitutes & infant sons	

Era: Kingdom

Story: 1 Kings 3 or 2 Chronicles 1:1–13 (Solomon's prayer); 1 Kings 10:1–13 or 2 Chronicles 9 (the queen's visit). Cited by Jesus: Matthew 12:42, Luke 11:31. See James 1:5–8.

Setting: By the time of King Solomon's reign, international commerce was thriving, with luxury items brought by land and sea from as far away as India. People paid high prices for imported products such as spices, precious stones, incense, gold, and woods for building and crafting beautiful instruments like harps. Trade routes plied along the Red Sea to Egypt to be shipped across the Mediterranean Sea or taken by caravans to Jerusalem. Control and upkeep of trade routes and tolls brought prosperity to nations through which goods passed or were transferred from one conveyance to another. It is thought that the kingdom of Sheba, centered in the southwest tip of the Saudi Arabian Peninsula (Yemen today), also encompassed parts of Ethiopia across the Red Sea. Frankincense then grew only in this region, and the Queen of Sheba brought a huge supply of the rare medicinal spice to Solomon.

King David had drawn the plans and located the products he needed for a grand house for the LORD, and he carefully tutored his son for his responsibility to build the Temple. The construction and furnishings of the famed Solomon's Temple required many trade agreements. By sea and land, word spread far and wide about Solomon's fabulous wealth, administrative skills, and judicial prudence. Adopting the terms of the covenant to bless all the nations, Solomon willingly offered his wisdom for the betterment of other nations—for which he was paid well.

Solomon contributed to several books of the Bible, and other parts are attributed to him. From these and similar writings arose the genre of wisdom literature. You will find Esther, Job, Psalms, Proverbs, Ecclesiastes, and Song of Solomon among the most readable books of the Hebrew Scriptures. They deal artfully with timeless concerns about life's meaning, common sense, destiny, suffering, guilt, and joy in "the fear of the LORD."[2]

Puzzler: The 31 chapters of Proverbs provide a monthly calendar of wisdom for orderly Bible reading. The structure of the two-part verses sharpens these nuggets of truth with primitive simplicity. Some proverbs will make you laugh; others will prick your conscience; and their vivid visual, auditory, and olfactory imagery keeps a steady parade on your mental screen like pop-up ads. Try your hand at composing your own proverb(s). How easy is that?

Elijah and the Widow of Zarephath: Distributions during Drought

PP, Elijah & widow of Zarephath	MS, widow of Zarephath & son

Era: Kingdom

Story: 1 Kings 17:8–24. Backstory: 1 Kings 16:29—17:7. Cited by Jesus: Luke 4:25–26. Widows and Jesus: Appendix B, #7, #26; Luke 18:1–8. Widows and the Church: Acts 6:1–7; James 1:27.

Setting: Survey the roles of prophets, priests, and kings (p. 45). Eleven times the summation of God's Law in Deuteronomy commands protection for widows, orphans, and aliens. Often this charge is linked to Israel's own sensitivities as defenseless slaves in Egypt. In the wisdom literature, Job, Psalms, and Proverbs reiterate concern for these three groups. Prophetic oracles advocate care for the widow, orphan, and alien and condemn nations who fail to do so. Prophets conveyed God's Word in vivid imagery and walked their talk in compelling action. This important office developed its identity primarily through schools of prophets. Prophets, including Jesus,[3] had the hazardous task of speaking truth to power, which earned them the wrath of exploitative leaders. Queen Jezebel's competing schools of prophets taught contrary to the covenant with the LORD (see the next story about Naboth).

Conflict with leadership would dominate Elijah's life. Ahab's wicked ways soon provoked Elijah's prediction of famine. He hurried *out of reach* to the east side of the Jordan, where he drank from a brook. God provided curbside food delivery by bizarre waiters. When the brook dried up, God told him to head northwest to the coast of the Mediterranean, where a widow in Zarephath would feed him. This took him directly into the neck of the woods where Jezebel's father ruled in Sidon. How odd of God to provide through a destitute widow. How could the hungry, hunted prophet *in reach of* his enemy dream of blessing this family?

Frankly, Elijah couldn't and didn't, but the God who once spread manna on the ground daily gave this alien widow, her indigent son, and her fugitive guest their daily cake. Alas, they did not live happily ever after. Ultimately cake could not sustain life. Only the prophet's vividly creative intervention brought both physical and spiritual awakening to this house. The LORD and Elijah fulfilled the covenant's stipulation to bless the nations with God's truth.

Puzzler: More than once even Jesus was amazed by the faith of Gentiles.[4] I raised my eyebrows at Elijah's impudent request to be fed first, even if that is still proper manners. Yet this runs parallel to Jesus's teaching to strive *first* for the kingdom of God, and all other needs will be supplied. When and why did you or someone you know sacrifice to the last bit of their resources? What happened afterward?

Naboth, Elijah, and Queen Jezebel: A Repellent Reputation

HW, Ahab & Jezebel	PP, Obadiah & Jezebel	PP, Jehu & Jezebel
PP, Elijah & Jezebel	PP, Naboth & Jezebel	PP, eunuchs & Jezebel
PP, the LORD's prophets & Jezebel	PP, leaders of Naboth's city & Jezebel	

Era: Kingdom

Story: 1 Kings 18–19, 21. See also 1 Kings 22:19–40 (Ahab's death); 2 Kings 2:1–18 (Elijah's departure); 2 Kings 9:30–37 (Jezebel's death). Ezekiel 46:18 states one lesson learned.

Setting: Review the stories of Ahab and Jezebel (p. 63) and Moses and the daughters of Zelophehad (p. 78). Intermarriage among local royalty may offer a less bloody way to gain a footing in a neighbor's territory than war, but not in this case. Such marriages introduced other gods that could erode faith in the invisible God of the Hebrews. Their faith was already weakened by the split of the northern kingdom of Israel from the southern kingdom of Judah ruled by David's line.

Queen Jezebel imported many prophets of Baal into Israel. Without protest from the Kings Ahab, son Joram (Israel), and Jehoram (Judah), the religion of their bloodthirsty wives won the day. The people of both Israel and Judah were torn between the LORD and Baal. It is little wonder that Elijah, the ardent prophet of the LORD, and his school of prophets irritated the royalty. The stories of this change agent for spiritual awakening and moral reform depict his compassion and courage followed by utter depletion and depression. In "the sound of sheer silence" or the King James Version's "a still small voice," God and the ministering angel gently healed his heart and redirected his energies. Note the specific ways God accomplished this turnaround in the physical, emotional, social, and spiritual domains. After Elijah's exit by a fiery chariot, Jehu, the hot-rodder, carried out his assignment to clean house with dispatch.

The Bible records only the following three notable interchanges between spouses: (1) David and Bathsheba about Solomon's accession to the throne, spurred on by the prophet Nathan; (2) Ahab and Jezebel about Naboth's vineyard, condemned by the prophet Elijah; and (3) Xerxes/Ahasuerus and Esther about Haman's evil plot, conveyed by the loyal eunuch Hathach.[5] In each one, a peer in the plot shaped the outcome at a crucial point in Hebrew history.

Puzzler: King David and Queen Jezebel sinned grievously. Both wanted what belonged to someone else, Bathsheba (p. 71) and a vineyard. Both killed the person who got in the way, Uriah and Naboth. Both used the hands of their subjects to carry out the murder. Why is David remembered with devotion while Jezebel garners notoriety? Don't be satisfied with the first answer that pops into your mind. Please keep in mind the hero of every Bible story.

Naaman and a Captive Girl: A Commander's Priceless Servants

PP, Aramean soldiers & Israelite girl	HW, Naaman & wife
PP, Naaman & Israelite girl	PP, King of Aram & girl

Era: Kingdom

Story: 2 Kings 5. Backstory: 1 Kings 19:19–21; 2 Kings 2. Cited by Jesus, Luke 4:27.

Setting: The Aramean king in the story was probably Ben-Hadad II, who ruled Aram in the mid-ninth century BCE. Ahab had worked out a peace agreement with Ben-Hadad, but boundary disputes arose after Ahab's death. Now his son by Jezebel, Joram, ruled in Israel and worshiped Baal. Children (and adults too frequently), then as now, often attributed almost magical skills to religious leaders. The leaders themselves might yield to the temptation to believe they in fact did possess supernatural powers. The worshipers in that agrarian region and era implored and appeased their deities in hopes for fertile land to feed their animals and people. Local gods ruled the literal earth their worshipers walked on, and crossing the border from one nation to another automatically transferred one to the local god in charge. Religions commonly required ritual washing for purification before worship. The beautiful Abana (today named Barada) and Pharpar Rivers flow near Damascus. And finally, the word "leprosy" was used in the Bible for any skin disease, not necessarily Hansen's Disease.

The heroine, whose innocent faith in Elisha occasioned the letter from Ben-Hadad to Joram on behalf of Naaman, had probably been orphaned by the invasion in which she was captured by the Aramean soldiers. I suspect she eventually learned what international hope and consternation her words stirred. Jesus received fury in his hometown by just mentioning this story and the one above about the faith of aliens. Local pride of homeland and office played right into the hands of anyone who preferred Naaman's death over his command in battle.

This story honored (unintentionally?) the LORD's commands to care for the widow, orphan, and alien. Naaman's wife did not become a *widow*. The *orphan* won the gratitude of her master and mistress. The *alien* Naaman secretly joined the fellowship of the Hebrews and the Almighty. In the muddy Jordan, he set aside his pride to heed the life-giving pleading of his servants. As usual, the true hero of the story is *the* Priceless Servant.

Puzzler: Elijah accepted the widow of Zarephath's last bit of food and hospitality. Elisha accepted the Shunammite couple's rooftop room (see Supplemental Stories ahead). Jesus accepted the support of people whom he had helped.[6] It was completely in order for prophets to receive gifts of gratitude. Yet here, Elisha refused Naaman's gifts, and his servant, Gehazi, received a sore reward for taking them. What made this situation different?

Supplemental Stories

Life, especially in our times, almost always requires people to deal with those outside their familiar extended family, their immediate community, and those featured in the media. Often our first response to these "strangers" falls short of compassion. Yet "You shall love your neighbor as yourself: I am the LORD" forever stands to prod people out of their comfort zones.

Joseph and Potiphar's Wife
Era: Founders. Story: Genesis 39–41 (part of larger story in 37–50).
Keep reading this famous story to see whether God's presence and revelations were worth the unjust price Joseph had to pay to preserve his trustworthiness before God.

Saul and Witch of Endor
Era: Kingdom. Story: 1 Samuel 28:3–25, 31:1–13.
The consequences of Saul's greed for booty and jealousy of loyal David yielded the terrifying absence of God. In desperate hopelessness, he turned to an outlawed medium.

David and Wise Woman of Tekoa
Era: Kingdom. Story: 2 Samuel 14:1—15:2.
David repeatedly failed to deal with his sons' crimes. The banished Absalom conspired to usurp the throne. Grief followed. How wise were Joab and the wise woman?

Elisha and Poor Widow, Rich Shunammite
Era: Kingdom. Story: 2 Kings 4:1–37, 8:1–6.
God's call to prophets urged concern for the widow, orphan, and alien. Elisha took this challenge to heart. What do his varied encounters show us about God's service?

Nehemiah and Queen
Era: Exile. Story: Nehemiah 1–2 and skim to the end.
Nehemiah's trustworthiness as cupbearer earned the king's and queen's confidence to grant his bold request. Despite obstacles, wit, wisdom, and wealth work wonders.

Men and Women Singers
Era: Exile. Story: Ezra 2:1, 41; Nehemiah 11:22–23, 12:27–43.
Recalling the plans of David and music director Asaph years before, two choirs led everyone in singing to celebrate rebuilding Jerusalem's walls. What music helps you rejoice?

10

Gospel Peers: Public and Powerful

This guidebook pays particular attention to one distinction between the sacred literature of other religions and the biblical record, its attention to women. Many women in the Old Testament have already been featured here. In comparison to surrounding cultures, women were highly valued even though they had limited choices about husbands, especially when political and economic gain motivated these decisions. To protect young women, the Law of Moses exacted stiff penalties from predators. The Hebrews kept careful records of family lines and approached the serious matter of selecting spouses thoughtfully. Two bases of this esteem derived from Genesis 1–3: (1) God's command to be fruitful and multiply and (2) God's promise that a seed of a woman would defeat the Archenemy. Women acquired status primarily through giving birth to many children, but barrenness brought distress and disgrace. Two other factors from the same chapters in Genesis were overlooked: (1) God's intention that partnership between man and woman reflect the image of God and (2) God's instruction for a husband to leave his family to be joined to his wife. The result empowered men over women.

But after all, hadn't the first woman unleashed death and evil into the world? *If* a woman's disobedience caused this great calamity, then it must also be asserted that *only* men killed God's Son, the solution to death and evil in the world. The Bible affirms neither assertion! Jesus and the authors of the Gospels balanced the books between men and women. Note that not one female numbered among Jesus's enemies who plotted for his execution, tortured him, and shamed him. Only one person, a woman, tried to save his life (see p. 66). The New Testament's portrayal of dynamics between genders changes dramatically for one reason.

Jesus loved women. This unmarried man made more women famous than anyone else in history, but he never drew attention to them for physical beauty, marriageability, or reproduction. Throughout the Gospels, women are portrayed positively except King Herod's wife and stepdaughter (see p. 38). In every encounter, Jesus elevated women for courage, faith, and devotion. He healed, taught, encouraged, and defended them.

All stories in this chapter take place in the era of the Incarnation. Appendix B lists all the stories in which Jesus interacted with women. These straightforward encounters endeared him to them and often puzzled or irritated the witnesses. Keep reading: the unsurpassed works of God with women and men are yet to be featured.

Visitors to Young Jesus and Mary: Treasures to Ponder

HW, Joseph & Mary	PP, shepherds & Mary	PP, King Herod & Mary
MS, Mary & Jesus	PP, wise men & Mary	PP, King Herod & mothers in Bethlehem

Stories: The famous Christmas pageant stories are in Matthew 2 and Luke 2:1–20, but it is also important to consider the full stories in Matthew 1:18–25 and Luke 1, 2:41–52.

Setting: Review Mary's Song (p. 4), the Herods (pp. 17, 38), Elizabeth (p. 46), and Mary and Joseph (p. 60). In the full accounts, note the voiced expectations of Messiah's deliverance. God had a different plan. The prominence of the *palace* in Matthew and the *Temple* in Luke set the scene; *government* and *religion* will collude to kill Jesus. Jesus's birth likely took place in the spring, when lambing ewes needed attention around the sun dial. Bethlehem, located in the verdant hills outside Jerusalem, supplied high-quality sheep used for sacrifices at the Temple, the supreme one being Jesus. No wonder that angels notified shepherds first. The arrival of the group of elite astrologers with their caravan of camels and servants made a notable stir in Jerusalem. Upon the family's return from Egypt, Joseph's skills in carpentry may have provided employment for him in the construction projects at Sepphoris, six miles northwest of Nazareth.

The couple probably stayed with their relatives in Bethlehem after Jesus's birth while Mary nursed and weaned him. This took enough time for King Herod to estimate up to two years for the new king's age. Fortunately, the little town probably had too few babies for Herod's butchery to be listed among his many cruelties in the contemporary historical accounts. But God took note and so did Mary.

The words and face of each treasured visitor were etched into her heart. Every character accepted God's invitation. For Joseph and Mary, obedience carried enormous difficulties. For Jewish shepherds, obedience took them across treacherous terrain in the dead of night. For Gentile wise men, obedience required months of travel. In every case, reaching their destination brought joy. Billions since then have done likewise.

Puzzler: See if you can still imagine being as excited as a child in anticipation of Christmas. In Luke 1–2, highlight forms of these five words: "favor," "joy," "glory," "praise," and "Holy Spirit." The Holy Spirit has access to your mind and heart and wants to deliver a message about Jesus, the climax of God's Grand Story. How curious and willing are you to let it seep deep into the core of your being? Try it. You might like it.

Simeon and Anna: News at the Temple

HW, Joseph & Mary	PP, Simeon & Mary	PP, Joseph & Anna
MS, Mary & Jesus	PP, Simeon & Anna	PP, Jesus & Anna
		PP, Luke & Mary

Story: Luke 2:21–40. Rituals after birth: Genesis 17:9–14; Exodus 13:1–16; Leviticus 12:1–8; Numbers 3:5–13.

Setting: The rituals surrounding birth reminded the Israelites of the covenant with the LORD, the delivery from slavery after the firstborn in every Egyptian family died, and the promise at a boy's birth of the Messiah to come. So that all could participate in sacred rituals, the Law provided a sliding scale of animals used for sacrifices. Joseph and Mary numbered among the poor who could offer only two turtledoves or two young pigeons to consecrate Jesus, the firstborn son. In Christianity, Jesus *is* God's firstborn son consecrated and sacrificed for humanity. As mentioned on page 47, Luke, the Greek-speaking Gentile doctor, may well have interviewed Mary in Ephesus for his stories of Jesus's birth. Luke wrote his Gospel and the Acts around the time of the destruction in 70 CE of the Temple. It was the setting of several significant events in Luke 1–2. There the religious authorities witnessed Jesus's first recorded words and his final controversies with them. As many Gentiles around the Mediterranean and into Asia became believers, the focus moved away from Jerusalem. Hearts that welcomed the Holy Spirit became the true temple rather than hewn stones decorated in gold.

Such were the hearts of all the characters listed at the top of the page. The presence of this baby boy unified the genders in attention to God's promise of the Redeemer. Twelve years later, the same family traveled to Jerusalem. When large groups traveled together, men separated from the women and children for conversation. Both Mary and Joseph may have thought "tweenager" Jesus was with the other group, so they did not miss him until the families regathered to sleep as night fell. I wonder if Simeon's sobering words about a soul-piercing sword came to the couple while they frantically searched for Jesus. Sadly, Anna and Simeon were no longer alive to look for him.

Puzzler: "Did you not know that I must be in my Father's house?" Jesus's first recorded words, a question (for us, too), do not refer to a place or building. The red letters in my childhood King James Version ring truer: "Wist ye not that I must be about my Father's business?" This twelve-year-old knew what met his desire and propelled his action. What actions and desires serve the "Father's business" in your life and work?

Disciples and the Syrophoenician/Canaanite Woman: Going to the Dogs

PP, disciples & woman	PP, disciples & woman's daughter
PP, Jesus & woman	PP, Jesus & woman's daughter

Story: Matthew 15:1–28, Mark 7:1–30. Backstory: Mark 3:7–11. Only a few miracles done for lack of faith: Matthew 13:53–58, Mark 6:1–6.

Setting: In diminishing order of insult, the archaic label "Canaanite" roused ancient hostilities; the broader term "Gentile" fixed a firm boundary; and "Syrophoenician" simply identified current locale. Matthew, Mark, and Luke tell many of the same stories, though sometimes in rearranged sequence. Not this time. The event followed on the heels of Jesus's controversial declaration about defilement. Rules about unclean food ensured that Jews and Gentiles would rarely share a meal together. We know of no instance of Jesus freely entering a Gentile's home. He healed them long-distance.[1] This Canaanite *mother* without status ranked at the bottom of the social and religious heap. The record cites three more children Jesus healed, each at the father's request.[2]

Jesus shocked his listeners by declaring all foods clean whether or not they were eaten with washed hands. Did not the primal defilement come from eating the forbidden fruit taken by Eve and Adam's pristine hands? Debunking a food taboo perplexed the disciples. So Jesus took them on a field trip where an "unclean" Canaanite woman's daughter "had an unclean spirit." When the mother's distress caused a ruckus, the disciples sniffed, growled, and barked for Jesus to get rid of her. The Greek word for dog indicates a little house pet, not a big mean dog. Who are the beloved pet dogs here, the woman or the disciples or both? And whose mouth(s) gave evidence of defilement?

Whether a child at the table or the puppy under it, it is hard to fathom the God who shows no partiality. Desperation shatters a sense of privilege. Our heads must bow to lick up the crumbs under the table. That's where Jesus met her eye to eye. When Jesus could not do miracles, the people were not in a position to recognize the healer under their table. Maybe this field trip resurfaced later at the Jerusalem Council (see p. 98).

Puzzler: Hindsight raises "what if?" and "if only" thoughts about this account. "Woman, great is your faith! Let it be done for you as you wish." What if Jesus had not traveled earlier to her region so she could hear of him? What if she had not persisted? What if the father had come instead? What if it had been her *son* who was troubled? If only Jesus hadn't sounded so tribal. How do details in this story give reasons to preserve it?

The Inhospitable Host and the Unwelcome Woman

PP, Jesus & woman	PP, Simon & woman	PP, guests and woman

Stories: Each Gospel reports a woman anointing Jesus. Luke 7:36–50 is a different story from John 12:1–8 (see p. 108) and from the nearly identical Matthew 26:6–13 and Mark 14:3–9.

Setting: This event took place during Jesus's early ministry in Galilee in the north, while the other three took place in Bethany, a village near Jerusalem in Judea in the south. Galilean crowds swarmed around Jesus to witness his healings and teachings. No doubt he and his disciples were welcomed into many homes. Hospitality had its protocols. Upon the arrival of a visitor, especially one as famous as Jesus, a servant would appear with a water bowl and towel to wash the dust and filth of the ground from the visitor's feet. Achy feet might be massaged if warranted. Cleansing oil might be offered to remove grit the wind lodged on face and beard. Once the guest was presentable, the guest and host would greet each other by exchanging kisses on both cheeks. The invited men then reclined on their left sides, head toward the table and feet extending away from it. Only the right (clean) hand touched the food. After the men had their fill, the women cleaned up and ate leftovers in the kitchen. Curious or hungry outsiders often loitered around the peripheries of courtyards at houses of prominent people. As a metaphorical aside, sheep selected for sacrifice in Jerusalem often arrived with cuts and sores on their feet. At the Temple their feet were anointed with oil as a salve for healing these blemishes.

The Pharisee had one objective for his invitation to Jesus: to test and judge him. A party crasher, an astonishingly bold woman of ill repute, played into his hands perfectly. Jesus noted his stony silence, raised eyebrows, and up-turned nose. Then Jesus turned the tables on the host by testing him with a disarming story that cornered the judge. Picture it: "Then *turning toward the woman,* [Jesus] said to [the Pharisee], 'Do you *see* this woman?'" (emphases mine).

Jesus equated the Pharisee's unwelcoming attitude to the woman with the host's treatment of himself. "Just as you did not do it to one of the least of these, you did not do it to me."[3] Since the Gospel records Simon's name, Luke may have interviewed him personally. This suggests that Simon took the parable to heart and recognized the theophany at his table as LORD. Commentators have gossiped for years about the identity of the woman. Does it really matter?

Puzzler: The indelible impression this story leaves convicts me of times I have entertained unwelcoming thoughts about someone, similar to those of Simon the Pharisee. How eager am I to welcome a change of heart in someone I do not like? Whether one has sinned much or little, "Lord, have mercy" rings celestial bells. The One Who Sees welcomes the uninvited and gives them peace. Forgiven! What impact does this story have on you?

Jesus and Salome, Mother of James and John: Clash of Kingdoms

PP, Jesus & Salome	PP, disciples & Salome	MS, Salome & James, John

Stories: Matthew 20:17–28. Mark 10:32–45 tells the same story without mentioning Salome. Luke 22:24–27 makes the point but with no names mentioned.

Setting: Salome may have been a sister or sister-in-law of Mary, mother of Jesus, and took part in the circle of women who cared so deeply about him that they were at the cross and at the tomb on Resurrection Sunday. Jesus gave Salome and Zebedee's sons James and John the nickname "Sons of Thunder." Jesus gave Andrew's brother Simon the nickname Cephas or Peter, which means "stone." Neither nickname suggests shy, docile, or malleable character but rather students that teachers keep within reach to squelch mischief. The two sets of brothers partnered in fishing businesses prosperous enough to permit them to leave their nets to follow the preacher John the Baptist, and then Jesus. Because Peter, James, and John are mentioned together in a handful of events, they became known as Jesus's inner circle.

Jesus habitually taught about the kingdom of heaven, and his miracles raised the disciples' hopes for positions of power when Jesus would usher it in. With throngs seeking him, ambition ran high in the dynamics among the disciples. However, this also contributed to their inability to pay attention when Jesus repeatedly told them he would be killed and rise on the third day. Since Peter was probably the oldest of the twelve disciples and the most likely to get into trouble for his impulsive questions and actions, it followed that the Sons of Thunder would stand at the head of the line for high ranks in the kingdom of heaven, right? Wrong! When Jesus washed the disciples' feet, Peter wondered at his master's action.[4] But when Pontius Pilate saw just a glimmer of Jesus's kingdom, the fearful governor tried to distance himself.[5]

Did the Sons of Thunder put their mother up to her request or was she the instigator? Only Matthew's Gospel mentions her role. That was not Jesus's assignment from his Father. Instead, he set them straight about competitive squabbling over position. In the end, it was King Herod who made sure that James was the first of the Twelve to enter the kingdom of heaven with high honors—at the edge of a sword.

Puzzler: Conscientious parents wish to help their children aspire to high endeavors. Salome's attempt to pull strings through her connection with Jesus can hardly be called wicked, and Jesus did not upbraid her for it. But his answer gives us pause about our own dreams and aspirations and those we pass on to the next generation. What petitions might Jesus welcome from you on behalf of your children (or of the next generation, for those without offspring)?

Peter and the High Priest's Servants: The Chargrill Charges

PP, John & woman at the gate	PP, Peter & woman at the gate	PP, Peter & servant-girl(s) at the charcoal fire

Story: John 13:36–38, 18:12–27, 21:1–19.[6] For conditions of the covenant with God see Leviticus 5:1 (refusal to act as a witness); Numbers 15:30–31 (intentional sin).

Setting: The Law defines guilt and determines sentence; it dispenses neither forgiveness nor mercy. In the early chapters of Leviticus, the Law of Moses provided for sacrifices to remedy for sins committed *unintentionally* or *in ignorance*. Intentional, defiant, and premeditated sinful actions had *no remedy*, no hope. The offenders' guilt remained, and the guilty were to be cut off from the people. While Roman law gave Jews exceptional freedom to practice their religion and govern their adherents, the death sentence could be enacted exclusive by Roman authority. No woman could appear in court for official testimony. Blasphemy was the only feasible charge against Jesus. The Jewish court charged him with blasphemy because he made himself Son of God, thus equal to God. Jewish officials then interpreted this to the Roman court as a charge of subversion against Caesar. Pilate stated the core issue here, "What is truth?"

Trauma may heighten one's recall or erase it. At the time of these events, John was probably a boy in his earliest two-digit years, when memory surpasses that at any other age. He was too young for cross-examination, and his connections made him an eyewitness. His account records the following italicized details not found elsewhere. *When Jesus washed the feet of the disciples, Peter objected to accepting this lowly gesture.* "*A detachment of soldiers*" together with the police from the chief priest and Pharisees" with Judas arrested Jesus in the Garden of Gethsemane. It was *Peter* who cut off the ear of *Malchus* at the arrest. Since John's family owned a business with a Judean branch, John was likely *the disciple who knew the High Priest and the woman at the gate. She permitted Peter to enter the courtyard and questioned him about knowing Jesus.* Therefore, this disciple witnessed Peter's denial. A *relative of Malchus* at the *charcoal fire had seen Peter at the garden.* In the other Gospels a servant-girl first questions Peter, then other bystanders. Now read Luke 22:59–62. The gut punch of a glance hits home.

Puzzler: In Jeremiah 17:9–10 the prophet wrote, "The heart is devious above all else; it is perverse—who can understand it? I the Lord test the mind and search the heart, to give to all according to their ways, according to the fruit of their doings." Trace Peter's actions in front of John, the women, and the bystanders. Assess whether the court trials Jesus underwent and the charcoal charges Peter denied mirror Jeremiah's description of the human heart.

Supplemental Stories

During the Incarnation era, a freshly formed family of brothers and sisters began to take shape. Neither blood ties nor sexual encounters brought them together; Jesus's transfiguring touch bonded them. When he took notice of the infirm, outcast, bereaved, and discounted, he endued them with the dignity of full membership in his family.

James, John, and Peter's Mother-in-Law
Story: Mark 1:29–31 (also Luke 4:38–39).
The Synoptic Gospels place healing her fever in Jesus's inaugural public ministry. Simon Peter's concern for his wife's family recalls an inaugural directive in Genesis 2:24.

Men of Sychar and Woman at the Well
Story: John 4:4–42, *note verses 39–42.*
In a culture that refused a woman's voice in court, the men hurried to check her source. Her meeting with Jesus readily authenticated her proclamation of astounding news.

Jesus and Bent Woman
Story: Luke 13:10–17.
Distraught that Jesus brought a woman into the men's turf at the synagogue, the leader complained. Jesus made nonsense of this objection, and the people rejoiced.

Religious Leaders and Widows
Story: Mark 12:38–44, Luke 20:47—21:4.
Disregard paragraph and chapter divisions that defeat the purpose of placing these incidents in juxtaposition. Jesus exposed the gaping chasm between greedy and generous hearts.

John and Mary
Story: John 19:25–30.
John only alludes to himself, but how like him to light up the love of Jesus for his mother at the finish line. How like God to welcome this son into the Holy Family.

Disciples and Women at the Tomb
Story: Matthew 28:1–10, Mark 16:1–14, Luke 24:1–12, John 20:1–18.
God entrusted women with the honor of heralding the Resurrection. Don't be too hard on disciples who scorned their news. Guess which two actually examined the evidence.

11

Early Church Peers: Productive and Persuasive

The stories featured in this chapter occurred in the Church era and come from Acts. Jesus left three promises to his disciples. First promise: He would be with them to the end of the age. In his company they learned to keep his command to love one another. This motivated sharing food, visiting prisoners, and collecting money from far-flung believers for their siblings suffering from famine in Jerusalem. Such love captured the attention of observers throughout the Roman Empire. Might the power of Christ's love be greater than the power of Rome's phalanx? A gathering, called a "church" of believers, named "Christians" (little Christs), welcomed once hostile Temple priests, God-fearers, sundry Gentiles, slave and free, male and female.

Second promise: The Holy Spirit would empower believers to spread the message of Jesus's life, death, and Resurrection to the ends of the earth. On the basis of what they had witnessed and the apt inspiration of the Holy Spirit, the once befuddled disciples became indefatigable apostles, the "ones sent forth." Luke's record in Acts narrates the sequence of events that indeed sent forth this message, termed the "Gospel" or "good news." Persecution, serendipitous encounters, visions, imprisonment, missionary trips, miracles, conversions, and court room defenses presented opportunities to proclaim the Gospel. From Pentecost onward, the Jewish founders of the Church taught not only what Jesus had said and done but also how he had fulfilled the prophetic oracles from previous centuries in ways no one had guessed. The startling conversion of Saul/Paul, the brilliant and belligerent Pharisee, galvanized understanding and application of God's Grand Story. Through his teaching during four missionary journeys, churches sprouted from local synagogues, forums, or homes. Whether received or resisted, the Gospel convinced minds and animated behavior. Never a dull moment!

Angels announced the third promise: Jesus would return someday from heaven. Years passed and original eyewitnesses began to die. Efforts turned to recording the story of Jesus for future generations awaiting his return. Starting in the 50s CE, Paul and other apostles wrote letters that were circulated among the churches. These epistles clarified the Gospel and addressed pastoral situations. The most reliable and helpful ones are preserved in the New Testament. The Gospels of Matthew, Mark, and Luke were completed around the time of the revolt in 70 CE against Rome, while John's Gospel and epistles took form about two decades later.

The apostles remembered the past by faith, motivated the present in love, and secured the future with hope. The Gospel's power to transfigure made saints from sinners. Despite the blood of countless martyrs and assorted efforts to obliterate the Bible, the gates of hell did not and shall not prevail against Christ's Bride, the Church. That's a promise, too.

The Hellenized Deacons and Widows: Continuity in Caring

PP, Hebraic apostles & Hellenized widows	PP, Hellenized deacons & widows
Apostles: Peter, John, James, Andrew, Philip, Thomas, Bartholomew, Matthew, James son of Alphaeus, Simon the Zealot, Judas son of James, Matthias (replaced Judas Iscariot)	
Deacons: Stephen, Philip, Prochorus, Nicanor, Timon, Parmenas, Nicolaus (proselyte)	

Story: Acts 6:1–7. Backstory: Acts 2:41–47, 4:32—5:11 (see p. 66). After-effects: Acts 6:8—8:40 (see p. 39 and the next story).

Setting: The early church began at Pentecost when Jewish pilgrims, dispersed through the three continents bordering the Mediterranean Sea, flooded into Jerusalem to celebrate Pentecost, or the Feast of Weeks (review p. 19). At the vast Temple courtyard, people gathered to socialize, hear the news, buy from merchants, discuss ideas from various teachers, and observe the hours of prayer. The visitors spoke Koine Greek, the language of commerce in the Roman Empire. Its simple grammar and structure made it easier to learn than classical Greek. The far-flung Jews rarely spoke the form of Aramaic used in Palestine, and only the literate followed the Hebrew readings at the synagogue. Palestinian women, largely confined to their homes, had scant skill in Koine Greek. The two language groups differed also in perspectives and attitudes.

After Pentecost, new believers gathered to learn from the apostles, pray, eat together, and participate in the earliest practices of breaking bread inaugurated by Jesus at the Last Supper. Widows numbered among hundreds of converts who remained in Jerusalem to learn about Jesus. Accommodations became cumbersome, especially for women by themselves. According to the covenantal priority of care for widows and aliens, the early church took responsibility for these Greek-speaking women. Language issues exacerbated perceived slights, and complaints escalated. Thus, the apostles had to address the new church's first internal problem.

Their solution came after much prayer and by the good will and wisdom of local Greek-speaking men, one of them not even Jewish-born. Ironically, two are known more for defending and spreading faith in Jesus than for aiding these widows. Lessons observed: man proposes, God disposes. God expanded the ministry of those with servant hearts, and many churches now take the names of the first Christian martyr, Stephen, and the first missionary, Philip.

Puzzler: At Pentecost thousands miraculously heard the Gospel in their mother tongue. Yet the first internal problem of the Church involved language differences between people of the same religion. Delegating men to serve food to women never caught on as a tradition in Christian fellowship. Since we can't count on miracles to solve our problems, how flexible are you in allocating your time, treasure, and talent to serve those in need?

The Chief of the Treasury and His Queen/Candace

PP, Ethiopian eunuch & Candace	FD, Philip & four daughters

Story: Acts 8:26–40; Isaiah 53 *note verses 7b–8c* (quoted). Backstory: Acts 6:1–7 (see previous story). After-effects: Acts 21:7–16 (see p. 39 and the next story).

Setting: The first-century term "Ethiopian" referred to a nation of very dark-skinned people in the upper Nile River region stretching northward from Khartoum to Aswan in current Sudan and southern Egypt. "Candace," the title for the queen mother, referred to the widowed wife of the late king and mother of the current king. Since the king was viewed as a god-like figure at that time in Ethiopia, he held authority over sacred matters while the Candace managed secular matters. Officials who rose to high rank under her authority had to be eunuchs. Volunteers for this procedure chose prestige over family life. Others had no choice. Jews abhorred this practice of mutilation and barred eunuchs from entering their worship. But Isaiah prophesied a time when God-honoring eunuchs would be welcomed.[1] Jewish law, monotheism, and wisdom held appeal for those who disdained the behavior of Greek and Roman gods. These God-fearers respected Judaism but were not willing or able to be Jewish proselytes. Also note that the act of reading was habitually performed aloud.

Spurred on by persecution in Jerusalem, Philip, one of the deacons, pioneered travel for evangelism. His family finally settled in Caesarea, where we met his four daughters with prophetic gifts. His service was a catalyst for outreach to the alienated, the Samaritans, and a eunuch who was a foreign dignitary. Philip must have absorbed the scriptural lessons that the risen Jesus opened to the couple going to Emmaus. On the spur of the moment, he immediately connected Isaiah's Suffering Servant with its fulfillment in Jesus centuries later.

I wonder if this brilliant chariot traveler and his interpreter read on to Isaiah 56, which addressed his own condition. He immediately responded joyfully to the good news that at last rendered this outsider a fully adopted child of God through the power of Jesus Christ. Like all believers, he had to work out how to bear that family name in his dealings with his Candace. The Holy Spirit's specialization in this and related matters is called sanctification.

Puzzler: Often Christians are accused of a holier-than-thou attitude by those who do not believe that Jesus is God. Christians may also receive patronizing comments and worse from those who scorn their beliefs and behavior. How might either of these situations have come into play between the Candace and the Chief of the Treasury? For help, check out the experiences of Daniel et al. with royalty and court officials (euphemism for eunuchs) in Daniel 1–6.

Peter and Rhoda: Holy Hilarity

MS, Mary, John's mother & John/Mark	PP, Peter & Rhoda
PP, Peter & Mary, mother of John Mark	bs, Joseph/Barnabas & Mary, his relative

Story: Acts 12. Backstories showing the influence of Barnabas: Acts 4:32–37, 9:26–31, 11:27–30. After-effects: Acts 13:1–5, and 15; Colossians 4:10; 2 Timothy 4:11; Philemon 24.

Setting: This event is the hinge on the door from a young church to a parent church that would spread around the world. Between the previous featured story and this account, the persecutor of the fledgling church, Saul/Paul, met the risen Jesus in a dramatic encounter and believed. Saul learned that he would carry the Gospel to the Gentiles, a daunting and dangerous calling. The nervous believers all feared him except for Joseph, rightly nicknamed Barnabas, "son of encouragement." Jesus may have included him among the unmarried pairs in the Seventy ambassadors (see p. 64). His relative Mary hosted Jesus and the early church on the spacious second floor of her home, the Upper Room. There Jesus washed his disciples' feet and celebrated Passover at the Last Supper. There the early believers often gathered to pray and welcomed the awaited Holy Spirit on Pentecost (review p. 19). The generosity and grace that Barnabas extended to Paul and to John Mark, even during conflict, spurred the Church's momentum. But the movement threatened the *status quo* jealously guarded by the elite. To nip the Church in the bud, religious leaders stoned Stephen. Herod Agrippa I (see p. 38) executed James, imprisoned Peter, and arrested others.

This tense situation called for a grave prayer meeting. Whenever Paul and Barnabas taught about prayer, this story no doubt brought the house down. In a jovial spirit of collegiality, they retold the tale of Peter flustering the undaunted Rhoda and shushing the utterly shocked prayer meeting. Their joy and relief not only elated them but also exposed their foibles in faith. Shaking his head, the prayer meeting host chortled, "Oh, we of little faith. God really pulled a joke on us." Instant hindsight bent them double with holy hilarity, and their sides ached with suppressed gales of graced laughter. As for their enemy, Herod Agrippa I's pride scorned a self-deprecating sense of humor.

The Cenacle (Upper Room), rich in memories though changed in appearance, remains an essential site for pilgrims in Jerusalem. More turning points there lie ahead.

Puzzler: A professor once quipped, "Praying is how we serve in the capacity of God's advisors." Please smile knowingly. Jesus focused prayer on "Thy kingdom come, thy will be done." Until then, Bernard of Clairvaux recommends seeking a higher degree of love (review p. 2). Learning to pray takes a lifetime. Try keeping a record of your prayers and outcomes. When have you been as dazed as Rhoda et al. by God's responsiveness?

Paul et al. and Lydia: A Man Calls, a Woman Answers the Door

PP, Paul with Silas, Luke, Timothy & Lydia	[PP, magistrates & Lydia]

Story: Acts 16:6–15, 40. The episode in the omitted verses is featured in the next story. Backstory: Acts 13–15. After-effects: Acts 20:1–6; Paul's letter to the Philippians.

Setting: Let's return to the Cenacle (see previous story) because this safe haven rich in memories also hosted momentous transitions ahead. Here the Church observed the focus move from Peter toward Paul, from Jerusalem toward Antioch, from predominance of Jewish toward Gentile believers. Here leaders developed protocol allowing Jewish and Gentile Christians to share hospitality (see pp. 28, 98). Throughout, Barnabas served side by side with Peter and Paul as catalyst, benefactor, preacher, teacher, conflict arbitrator, donation amasser, and travel companion. Mission trips followed a pattern. A pair or more of apostles traveled to a new city, where they penetrated the synagogue with the Gospel. Soon God-fearing non-Jews joined the group of new Christians. As the good news spread into the wider community, other Gentiles became Christians. However, Jewish opposition often forced Christians out of the synagogue. Gentile hostility could lead to arrest and imprisonment. Before departing, the apostles selected leaders for the new church. Supportive travel partners stayed behind, and others prepared the way at the next city on the itinerary. The apostles wrote epistles to the churches to encourage and guide practice of faith. On his next journey, Paul revisited each church in person.

Philippi achieved fame for its dyeing works, especially royal purple (crimson) to outfit legions and dignitaries. Not even a quorum of ten men for a synagogue lived in this Roman colony for retired military. Because of the priority of avoiding even the appearance of sexual motivation for missions, God wisely sent a *man* in a vision to issue the invitation, even though a God-fearing *woman*, a merchant of purple, led the response to the Gospel.

Without the vision, the apostles would have discounted Philippi as fertile soil to plant the Gospel seed. Their plan to travel northeast closed down, and the vision directed them northwest. Paul's epistle to the Philippian church exudes rejoicing, unity, hope, love, gratitude, and counsel. Writing from house prison, he records an early hymn (2:6–11) and reflects on his own personal journey into faith (3:4–14). Treasure this jewel box of pastoral wisdom from Paul.

Puzzler: The apostles used no gimmicks, sales pitches, or clever jingles in their teaching. The miracles affirmed their message and offered concrete signs of the reality of God's power and promises for believers. They did endeavor to adapt their presentation of the Gospel to the backgrounds of their audiences. What biblical and other stories bond with your background? How have these stories influenced you when circumstances summoned them?

Paul, Silas, and the Fortune Teller: Freed from Three Possessions

PP, owners & slave-girl	HW, jailer & wife	[PP, magistrates & Lydia]
PP, Paul, Silas & slave-girl	PP, Paul, Silas & jailer's wife	PP, Paul, Silas & Lydia

Story: Acts 16:16–40. Backstories: Acts 15 *note verses 19–21, 29* (conclusions of the Jerusalem Council); Acts 16:1–15 (Lydia's conversion and hospitality).

Setting: The Jerusalem Council paved the road to ministry in Gentile cities like Philippi. After listening to reports, silence, prayer, and confirmation from Scripture, James, the half-brother of Jesus and leader of the Jerusalem church, issued four stipulations enabling Jews and Gentiles to offer each other accommodations in good conscience. Dietary laws about blood were known in every city where Jews resided but may need explanation today. In Jewish tradition blood carried God-given life. At Passover, its power on Hebrew's doorposts had protected the Hebrews. In sacrifices, its use symbolized atonement wrought by substitution of animal's blood for human blood. Animals were beheaded rather than strangled to minimize suffering and drain blood efficiently. Any vestige of idolatry was repugnant. Fornication would strain the integrity of church contacts when men and women prayed and served together.

In accepting hospitality, Lydia, Paul, and company confirmed their willing compliance with these practical stipulations. Even with Lydia's accommodations and the new church's support, Paul and Silas still ended up in prison. The problem occurred when a fortune-telling "spirit" spoke through a slave-girl. Accurate divinations from her involuntary mouth made her owners rich. However, the apostles detested advertisement, even though the words were true, from this disruptive speaker that craved to drown out the internal persuasion of the Holy Spirit in the hearts of the Philippians. When Paul carried out exorcism, the girl was freed from possession by (1) this agitating spirit and (2) her masters.

When the furious owners' stock crashed, they devised a way to take vengeance on the apostles. Soon Paul and Silas found themselves in the possession of (3) the local jailer, but the Holy Spirit took charge. Also, I conjecture that Lydia's quick thinking, influence, and generosity enabled her to pull some strings on behalf of the apostles and the ex-slave. In any case, two households, two men, and two women could sing joyfully in Philippi.

Puzzler: (1) Judaism's moral code commanded wide respect, but Jesus was convicted of blasphemy for declaring that he and God were one. (2) Roman law outshone that of any previous government, but Jesus was executed by a Roman governor. Paul and Silas (3) conducted themselves honorably and (4) insisted that the magistrates exonerate them publicly. Then or now, weigh the import of these four factors in a decision to accept or reject the Gospel.

Paul, Apollos, and Priscilla: Teachers during Turbulence

PP, Paul & Priscilla	HW, Aquila & Priscilla	PP, Apollos & Priscilla

Story: Acts 18:1—19:1. See Romans 16:3–5 (opposition from outside); 1 Corinthians 1–4 (internal disunity); 1 Corinthians 16:12, 19 and Titus 3:13 (co-workers). Survey this couple on page 65.

Setting: The changing population of the expanding church presented challenges in language, leadership, and loyalty. The early church quickly addressed the problem of fair food distribution (see p. 94). Integrating Gentiles and Jews in the church presented thornier issues (see previous story). Rome permitted other religions and gods as long as they gave ultimate loyalty to the emperor, but Jewish staunch monotheism historically refused to bow to any other god. However, Roman and Jewish leaders negotiated for Judaism to be awarded the status of a protected religion. While Jews worshiped in a temple built by the Roman King Herod the Great, Jewish zealots in Palestine stood ready to lead guerilla attacks. Expansion of the Gospel beyond Palestine drew the attention of officials. At first, Rome considered Christianity a cult within Judaism. But at Philippi and elsewhere, a Gentile majority eating with Jews to worship a risen Jesus looked like a new religion. Loyalist Jews stirred up riots that Roman officials had to quell. Both groups saw the church as a *threat*. Eventually Christianity lost its protected status.

The church at the home of Priscilla and Aquila spread its influence throughout Asia. From Peter at Pentecost and onward, Paul, Barnabas, Priscilla, Aquila, and Apollos taught, reasoned, encouraged, convinced, examined evidence, and argued persuasively to affirm the Jewish roots of Christianity, and the Jerusalem Council's stipulations guarded Jewish traditions. On the other hand, some traditionalists thought Gentiles had to become Jews before they could be Christians. The apostles united to denounce this notion.

Some believers naturally identified with a specific apostle. This led to divided loyalties as members of each group each claimed and proclaimed its own pet leader. Slow down to read Paul's teaching about this problem in 1 Corinthians 1–4. The works of love we construct to the glory of the Triune God and in service to others display degrees of luster or lackluster. Here's Paul's rating scale analogy: gold, silver, precious stones, wood, hay, and straw.

Puzzler: To worship their gods, the ancients constructed marble temples that have lasted two millennia. Annually thousands travel to savor the beauty that even their ruins display. By contrast, the Holy Spirit, whose breath gave humans an *eternal* soul, invites us to offer our bodies as temples for the Spirit's dwelling. Appraise your temple's durability and purpose on Paul's rating scale. How does that impact your net worth from God's perspective?

Supplemental Stories

This family of sons and daughters of God, like blood-related families, has squabbles over big and small matters. Unlike blood-related families, it includes several mothers and fathers, plus brothers and sisters with social class, ethnic, status, and educational differences. Watch these people with diverse backgrounds learn to live as members of Jesus's household.

Leading Men and Devout Women

Story: Acts 13:13–52 *note verse 50.*
Jealousy will reveal one's actual spirituality. These troublemakers incited a pivotal point in church history when Paul and Barnabas walked out on habitually devious objectors.

Paul, Apollos, Peter, and Chloe

Story: 1 Corinthians 1:4–17, 3:1–9, 4:6–7.
"A little bird told" Paul about things said behind the backs of church leaders. He identifies her and writes a letter to correct the situation in a Christ-centered way.

Paul and Co-workers

Story: Romans 16:1–16.
No meeting of early church workers that intentionally excluded one gender is recorded in the Bible. Find ten women in Paul's greetings here. Appendix C lists more.

Clement, Epaphroditus, and Euodia, Syntyche

Story: Philippians 4.
These co-workers provided food for Paul in prison and help with other needs. In times of high stress, their relief made his writing possible, to the benefit of the Church and the world.

Timothy and Widows, Spiritual Mothers, Sisters

Story: 1 Timothy 5:1–16; Titus 2:1–8.
Paul's instructions to his assistants contrasted devoted mothers and sisters in the church with fickle freeloaders who took advantage of the church's generosity.

Philemon, Paul, Onesimus, and Apphia

Story: Philemon.
This masterpiece of Christian diplomacy addresses the thorny issue of a runaway slave and his master, both now Christians, while a church leader, sister Apphia, looks on.

The Hebrews et al.

The early church forged affiliations among all sorts and conditions of believers in the following sampling of categories: (1) married, (2) single or widowed, (3) highly educated, (4) skilled labor, (5) wealthy, (6) poor, (7) Palestinian Jews, (8) Hellenized Jews in Jerusalem, (9) Jews of the diaspora, (10) mixed heritage, (11) non-Jewish God-fearers, and (12) Gentiles.[1] From Pentecost on, the increasingly multicultural church brought diverse men and women together as peers not connected by sexual or blood ties. Their questions helped the apostles to clarify matters of faith and practice. Their objections challenged the apostles to forge links from their hearers' backgrounds to Jesus and vice versa. Their curiosity increased appreciation for the symbolism of Jewish history and traditions that Jesus had acknowledged. Their spiritual hunger was satisfied by the ways Jesus fulfilled the longings of Moses, psalmists, and prophets about the promised Messiah. Their hope for life beyond life piqued interest in the death, Resurrection, and Ascension of Jesus. Whether at the Cenacle, in a chariot, by a riverside, on Mars Hill, at court, or in prison, the Holy Spirit guided these conversations that yielded a growing harvest of Christians.

With this diversity in mind, may I ask who wrote what has been called the Letter to the Hebrews? The major candidates are Paul, Barnabas, and Apollo. Barnabas, the consummate encourager and bridge builder, grew up in the shadow of the High Priest's palace. Paul from Tarsus came to Jerusalem as a young man to be taught by the leading Jewish scholars. Apollos from Alexandria may never have visited Jerusalem. This talented trio could speak to Jews, Gentiles, and everybody in between as carriers of both a heritage of an insider looking out *and* the perspective of an outsider looking in. Hebrews 13:18 states: "Pray for *us*; *we* are sure that *we* have a clear conscience, desiring to act honorably in all things" (emphases mine). The use of *I* and *me* that follows concerns a meeting with the recently released Timothy and the author. In 1 Corinthians 16:12 Paul reports such a delay when Apollos could not visit Corinth at the time of Paul's request.

Therefore, this seminal manuscript, "Hebrews et al.," represents a number of contributors, including countless unnamed seekers, whose attention to the Gospel widened comprehension of God's Grand Story. Then and now this document masterfully presents the supremacy of Jesus Christ not only to Hebrews but also to millions grafted into that family tree. Undoubtedly the author(s) addressed it to the world at large. If Apollos finally compiled it, Priscilla and Aquila's instruction from Paul and various seekers runs throughout it. BTW, when they looked around the table for a secretary, Priscilla naturally got volunteered. Right?

PART V

GOD'S GRAND STORY: CLIMAX AND CULMINATION

Anticipate slowing down to savor the incomparable stories featured in this climactic chapter. These narratives bursting with life may broaden your readiness for willing suspension of disbelief or raise your level of skepticism. The accounts inevitably raise the question, who is this man, Jesus? Comparisons ran wild in observers' heads. Guilt-ridden King Herod almost hoped that Jesus was actually John the Baptist resuscitated. Since angels are messengers of God, was Jesus greater or less than an angel? Was he a reincarnation of the prophet Jeremiah? Had Elijah returned as promised? Could Jesus have done miracles by the power of Satan?

No writer of fiction wishing to be believed would have risked the role reversals that appear in these accounts. Why would men, not women, prepare this dead body of a condemned criminal for burial, especially when this act would make these religious officials unclean during Passover and the sabbath? Unthinkable! In a culture where women's testimonies were not recognized in court (and elsewhere), how ludicrous would it be for women, not men, to proclaim the good news. Moreover, how could the women's doubtful account make martyrs, usually men, willing to die? Impossible! Such tales would make blatantly faulty *fiction*, indeed.

Nevertheless, the spices Nicodemus donated let the women keep theirs for later martyrs. Knowledge of the Resurrection spread through efforts by unconnected men and women who could neither coordinate nor guess the impact of their actions. Unbeknownst to them, God designed it that a first fruit of the kingdom of God would be blended efforts of both genders toppling stereotyped sex roles without apology. Adam and Eve crashed cymbals to celebrate, and these saints kept marching to a different drum. They knew why Good Friday was good.

12

The Summit of the Story: Cosmic Countdown

The featured stories in this chapter trace a cosmic countdown in God's Grand Story: *three* resuscitations; *two* fragrant bookends of the Passion account; *one* victory over death.

This chapter cites all ten resuscitations in the Bible and features the three in the record that Jesus accomplished. Compare his with those recorded in the Old Testament and later ones in Acts. Jesus's resuscitations demonstrated his capacity to regenerate life. Jesus promised his followers abundant life *now* and eternal life *to come* with a prepared place in his kingdom. Could he really deliver on such extraordinary promises? How could the disciples know? Jesus could expect these honest questions. The resuscitations were forerunners of what would shock and convince them that Jesus was not only telling the truth but also the actual source of life.

The climax in God's Grand Story occurred during the last week of Jesus's life, known as Holy Week or the Passion. Every Gospel devotes a hugely disproportionate segment of its account to these few days, and the Passion cannot be overestimated. Follow Jesus's controversies with the religious leaders, betrayal, Last Passover Supper, arrest, trials, and execution by reading the entire account in at least one of Matthew 21–27, Mark 11–15, or Luke 19:28—23:56. Then meditate upon John 12–19. Young John, the only eyewitness among the Twelve, gives details not recorded elsewhere. In his reflections in old age, he could safely name people now dead: Nicodemus (see p. 109), Lazarus, Malchus (see p. 91), Clopas, and Mary, the wife of Clopas (see Appendix B, #31). He omitted some incidents the other Gospels had circulated for years and added Jesus's cherished assurances just before his death.

The next two featured stories present the fragrant bookends enclosing the events that provoked and effected the execution of Jesus. His words and actions immortalize the fragrance of sacrificial love. The fourth story happened six days before Passover at the home of Mary, Martha, and Lazarus in Bethany. The Passion begins with Mary of Bethany's perfume lavishly poured on Jesus that infuriated Judas. Afterward, he headed to the religious leaders to make a deal to betray Jesus for thirty pieces of silver. The fifth story takes us to the newly cut tomb of Joseph of Arimathea. The shroud donated by this Sadducee and the spices costing a fortune offered by Nicodemus, a Pharisee, were used when they prepared Jesus's body for burial. Thus the pattern continues of devoted women and men appearing at crucial pivotal points in God's Grand Story. As you read and review the accounts of this most sacred time called Holy Week, observe the parts men and women played. We will return to those observations.

The culminating story here began at dawn on the first day of the week when women carrying spices went to the tomb. It was empty! The Resurrection accounts suggest that Jesus departed like a butterfly vacating its cocoon. Jesus never walked off with anything he hadn't paid for so he left the tomb, the grave clothes, and the spices behind. The aroma of the hundred-pound bouquet still wafted from the linens. The Resurrection of Jesus was of a different order altogether from resuscitations. Those resuscitated bodies eventually died. Usually bodies decayed in a trench grave. Wealthy families laid the wrapped body on a slab in a stone cut tomb. After a year, any remaining bones were sealed in a container called an ossuary. Criminals' bodies were dumped in a smoking heap outside the walls of Jerusalem where predatory animals consumed them. By contrast, Jesus's body was spared decay and was resurrected an immortal body, recognized by his voice and by the scars of his crucifixion. Government and religious authorities had custody of his body and guarded it carefully, but they could never produce it to disprove the apostles' claims that they had seen the risen Christ and had eaten with him.

The Only Son of a Widow at Nain: A Simple Story

MS, widow & only son	PP, Jesus & widow

Era: Incarnation; Kingdom in reviewed story

Story: Luke 7:11–17. Survey Elijah and the widow of Zarephath, 1 Kings 16:29—17:24 (p. 81). Note similarities and differences between the two situations.

Setting: Generally Jews highly respected the human body as God's creation, and they guarded the dead against dishonor such as being neglected, dismembered, mutilated, or left to lie or hang exposed overnight. Touching a dead body made a person unclean for gathered worship. While men could clean and prepare a man's body for burial, women normally did this work for both genders. As already mentioned, the common people in Jesus's day held simple burials no more than a day after death. Trenches were dug where a corpse, not always in a coffin, was laid and covered over to a sufficient depth to conceal the odor of decomposition (which could be very rapid) and to protect the body from carrion-feeders. Villagers processed with the bereaved family as the body was carried on a pallet to the burial place. Professional mourners might weep, cry, recite, or sing laments on this final journey.

Only Luke, the Gentile, records this resuscitation. In his sequence, Jesus had just preached a shorter version of the Sermon on the Mount, which in Matthew 5–7 is a record length of red print in red-letter editions. In it, Jesus encouraged being kind and loving toward enemies. To illustrate, he immediately entered Capernaum, a fishing seaport, to heal a highly valued servant of an unusually well-liked Roman centurion whose faith and diplomacy amazed him. Then the crowd followed him *to* Nain, where they met a crowd processing *from* Nain with the body of a widow's only son. No status or pulling of strings here. You already know the outcome, but don't overlook the details. With so many witnesses, word spread like wildfire.

The unembellished simplicity of this story raises the curtain on an ample stage for an active imagination to play many characters: a desperate woman left without resources wonders what she has done to deserve this; her son awakens to an exuberant command and wonders who this stranger is; a betrothed woman beholds her shattered future reassemble and wonders if this new man's desire remains steadfast; and a frowning skeptic tries to figure out the trick.

Puzzler: Proverbs 8:30–31 says wisdom was the daily delight of the Creator "like a master worker ... rejoicing in his inhabited world and delighting in the human race." An unsolicited act of God's compassion and grace, unearned and unexpected, can transfuse joy throughout one's psyche and spirit. We are always *on the receiving end* of the divine gift of joy. For just a moment try to conceive what Jesus experienced *on the giving end* of joy.

Jairus and the Hemorrhaging Woman: A Complicated Story

PP, Jesus & woman	PP, physicians & woman	PP, Jesus & Miss Jairus
FD, Jairus & daughter	HW, Jairus & wife	PP, 3 disciples & Mrs. Jairus
PP, Jairus & woman	PP, Jesus & Mrs. Jairus	PP, 3 disciples & Miss Jairus

Era: Incarnation; Kingdom in reviewed story

Story: Matthew 9:18–26, Mark 5:21–43, Luke 8:40–56. See also Leviticus 15:25–33 (discharges that render one unclean). Survey Elisha and the Shunammite woman (p. 84).

Setting: The ruler of a synagogue oversaw all its elders and functions, including civil government, worship, and schooling. Only a scholar or national hero commanded more attention and esteem. For centuries it had been known that body fluids carried diseases. Touching a bleeding person, a dead body, or a woman during menstruation made a person unclean. Both persons who were unclean because of their own body fluids and those unclean for touching such persons could not attend worship and other functions at the synagogue until the situation had cleared for an allotted time. A synagogue ruler exercised authority to discipline violators, and punishment might include excommunication and scourging. In the minds of Jews and early Christians, the number twelve immediately recalled the twelve tribes of Israel, sons of Jacob, and the Twelve, disciples of Jesus, respectively. Numerology mattered.

Jairus and his wife treasured their only child, a twelve-year-old daughter. Their prestige and esteem had already turned the eyes of young men awaiting Jairus's favor for the girl's hand. Meanwhile despite many ineffective treatments, an unclean woman steadily declined for twelve years from a flow of blood. Desperate situations in both houses brought Jairus and the woman together at Jesus's feet, two beggars. They were inextricably linked because Jairus held sole authority to open the synagogue to her. The patient gentleman listened while the unclean outcast spilled out her sad story. This delayed Jesus from arriving at Jairus's house on time, or so it appeared. How could Jairus determine the truth of the woman's claim that her very private illness was healed? Fury would boil at the synagogue if she dared to appear.

Jesus said their courageous faith in him, not a magical touch of his garments or hands, brought healing. By faith the hemorrhaging woman risked breaking the Law, and Jairus risked losing his reputation.

Puzzler: Imagine the collective gasp when Mrs. Jairus, the outcast, and Miss Jairus enter the women's section at the synagogue together. Jairus faces the people up front to speak. Israel and many more spend all they have to appease the gods. Yet we still hemorrhage hatred, loneliness, poverty, conflict, injustice, etc. But now the death and restoration of an only-begotten child allow her father to welcome lawfully those once unclean. Uncover the Gospel here.

Lazarus and Welcoming Sisters: The Turning Point

PP, Jesus & Mary	PP, disciples & the sisters	PP, mourners & the sisters
PP, Jesus & Martha	BS, Lazarus & Mary, Martha	

Era: Incarnation

Story: Luke 10:38–42 (the spat); John 11:1–44 (the grave exit) and 11:45–57 (the fallout). More from this family comes in the next story.

Setting: The town of Bethany was less than an hour's walk from Jerusalem. Houses of the affluent often had a central open-air courtyard surrounded by the living quarters. The kitchen area included food and wine storage rooms and an outdoor oven behind and out of sight of the courtyard where guests gathered to eat. A servant met the invited guests and washed their dusty feet. Neighbors and party crashers might enter the courtyard from the street. As now, the host might greet male guests with a kiss on both cheeks. Mourners gathered in the courtyard to comfort the bereaved. They might arrive with food in hand to relieve the family members of the chores of food preparation and entertaining. The family tomb might be a distance away where a cliff, natural stone, or a shelter could be cut to house the slabs on which to lay a body. It would have been wrapped tightly with strips of cloth, sometimes with spices placed between the layers to mask the odor of decay. If the tomb was spacious, mourners could enter to sit with the body of their loved one.

You know the contentment of returning home after a busy day, week, or month away. Hounded by officials and surrounded by supplicants all day, Jesus craved a space to dine with his disciples in privacy and to rest in ease. Mary, Martha, and Lazarus offered Jesus that kind of hospitality after his labors in Jerusalem. These close friends ungrudgingly took his banter about the sisters' contrasting ways of showing their affection for their trusted friend.

How strange for Jesus to delay in coming to their aid when the sisters called upon him in desperation. But he had two greater objects in mind: the glory of his Father and the culmination of his mission. The consequences of the definitive sign revealed at this home hurtled all of them into his final week. When Lazarus's presence brought down threats on his life, this trio of sibling solidarity could point confidently to living proof for hope that death is not the end.

Puzzler: Few biblical narratives probe "what if?" and "if only" queries as poignantly as this one. During the discussion about heading off to see the deathly ill Lazarus, Thomas, whose glass was (almost) always half empty, opined, "Let us also go, that we may die with [Jesus]." Was their trip to Bethany worth it? How do you decide whether to stay put or to risk setting sail in seas that hide physical, financial, emotional, or spiritual icebergs?

Judas and Mary of Bethany: The Clash of Generosity and Greed

PP, Jesus & Mary	PP, Jesus & Martha	BS, Lazarus & sisters
PP, Judas & Mary	PP, disciples & Mary	

Era: Incarnation

Story: John 12:1–11. Backstory: John 11. The nearly identical passages in Matthew 26:6–16 and Mark 14:3–11 may refer obliquely to this incident.

Setting: These three accounts mention both the controversy about the woman's lavish gift and its connection to Jesus's burial. They diverge on what was anointed, his head or his feet. Anointing the head with oil traditionally signified a rise to the throne or a call to a solemn and sacred task. The oil symbolized the Holy Spirit's empowerment for the calling. Fragrance drew attention to the otherwise commonplace gesture of washing a guest's feet. Note that in this case, Mary is one of the gathered disciples even though the custom called for men and women to eat separately, men first, with leftovers for women and children. Though Martha is serving, she also participates in the group. These close friends apparently continued to adopt Jesus's invitation for women to join the men at the table. People with leprosy, a term used to cover Hansen's Disease and other skin afflictions, were forced to live in groups away from the population. Fear of hereditary or contagious skin diseases could discourage marriage to their children.

If the three accounts report the same event, Simon of Bethany who suffered from leprosy was the isolated father or deceased ancestor of the three siblings. This may explain why they appear to have been unmarried. When Caiaphas, the high priest, decided Lazarus and Jesus must die, a menacing shadow fell over the home that had offered sanctuary to Jesus. But once more they risked a visit. Martha's gracious hospitality and Mary's lavish generosity endued this evening with fragrance in honor of their cherished guest. The time was right.

Jesus knew his hour had come. Mary's intuitive gift heated Judas's jealousy into a flame of spiteful and greedy vengeance. This pivotal clash of passions set in motion a sequence of events that would not be halted. The tomb in Bethany foreshadowed another tomb in Jerusalem. Both burst open. The first tomb hinted at the hope that the second tomb confirmed. That hope shall never be halted.

Puzzler: With choosing not to love come isolation and loneliness. With choosing to love come joy and grief. When Jesus wept at the tomb in Bethany, he groaned in anger that raised its fists at the carnage of death. Yet Jesus thrust upon his dear friend, Lazarus, the destiny of dying twice. The loyal Lazarus responded with the Aramaic equivalent of "No problem, Master. Been there, done that." What image and caption would you put on his grave tee shirt?

Joseph of Arimathea, Nicodemus, and Watching Women: A Royal Burial

PP, Joseph of Arimathea & watching women	PP, Nicodemus & watching women

The only named women are Mary Magdalene and Mary the mother of Joses.

Era: Incarnation

Story: Matthew 27:57–66, Mark 15:42–47, Luke 23:50–56, and John 19:38–42. Read at least two accounts for added details. Backstories of Nicodemus: John 3:1–21, 7:37–52.

Setting: Sadducees and Pharisees made up the Jewish ruling body, the Sanhedrin (review p. 17). Though it was not democratic, members did voice their views, cast their votes on issues, and administer most matters. However, the king appointed an acquiescent high priest. Bolstered by Rome's exclusive authority to impose the death penalty, officials were unbending about law and order and kept radical political and religious groups at bay. Men grieving at a crucifixion risked being arrested as co-conspirators. While women could not witness in court, they could publicly grieve at the cross. For centuries women had spun linen grave cloths to prepare bodies for burial. Since spices had to be imported, the cost of transport and trade made some spices literally worth more than their weight in gold. Women purchased the amount of spice they could afford to spread in the body wrappings.[1] Touching a corpse made one unclean for seven days.

In the minority on the question of Jesus, at least two men on the Council shared a quiet, secret, longing for God's reign on earth embodied in the actions and teaching of Jesus. When Jesus was condemned to death, the elder Joseph of Arimathea, a Sadducee, and the younger Nicodemus, a Pharisee, searched their souls, did some quick thinking, and took action. There might be trouble when the city learned the prophet had been crucified. They had at most five hours till sundown when Jerusalem closed down for sabbath. The elderly Joseph had prestige and political clout with Pilate, and at his prime, Nicodemus had physical strength and quick access to goods. They met at Joseph's newly cut tomb near the crucifixion site. Thanks to this bipartisan team, no birds and dogs would eat Jesus's body or drink his blood. Their deed was reported, and the two headed home to self-isolate for seven days.

Did the weary men see a few women across the way watching the tomb? God did.

Puzzler: The unique role for Joseph of Arimathea in God's Grand Story coalesced in *one afternoon* of his long life. His secret faith, his position, his age, his wealth, his new tomb near the crucifixion site, his colleague, and his respect for Jesus converged "for such a time as this." Now Esther smiles. Would you consider it a loss if your life in its entirety focused in the events and decisions of one day? How can one be ready for such an occasion?

Peter, John, and Various Women: The Empty Tomb

PP, Peter, John, and disciples & women from the tomb	PP, Jesus & women at the tomb

Named women include Mary Magdalene, Mary mother of James, Joanna, and Salome.

Era: Incarnation

Story: Matthew 28:1–15, Mark 16:1–8, Luke 24:1–12, and John 20:1–23. Eyewitnesses may recall different details; identical testimonies may indicate collusion. (Review pp. 5–8.)

Setting: The tomb of a wealthy person was cut into stone to make a small cave with a low opening for the entrance of the body and a slab where it was laid. Enough room might be left for mourners to sit with the body. Outside the tomb, a large rolling stone stood in a slightly sloped groove. Rolling it *down* secured the opening and barred intruding animals and humans. Rolling it *up* the groove to reenter the tomb would be exceedingly toilsome.

The accounts emphasize that the women who observed the location of the tomb had come from Galilee with Jesus. They did not expect him to die, so they would not have carried burial spices. The length of time the unknown men and their servants were at the tomb indicated that they were wrapping the body. At least two women remained at a discreet distance from the tomb while other women hurried to the market to buy spices before the sabbath began. The male disciples in hiding may have added to the purse. The exhaustion of the long night and shock of their master's crucifixion had traumatized them. Their minds had been full of dreams of the high positions they would hold in Jesus's kingdom. The prediction Jesus made that he would die and rise again in three days did not even register with them.

But the religious leaders did remember what Jesus had said. They had misconstrued it to use against him during questioning before the Sanhedrin. Therefore, they wanted to be sure the body did not disappear and asked Pilate for help. But Pilate, who had not wanted to execute him, had washed his hands of the matter and was eager to close the files on the case. He told them to handle their religious concerns on their own nickel.

When the women broke the news of the empty tomb, the disciples thought the women were in hysterics. Finally, Peter and John went to the tomb to see for themselves. Meanwhile, Joseph of Arimathea and Nicodemus ruminated about the blood on their unclean hands.

Puzzler: Rome crucified thousands, and people regularly saw death closer up than most of us ever will. Judas had committed suicide. On that singular first day of the week, these women and men were not expecting to see Jesus, *and* they did not doubt that they had seen him. They had no time for gullibility and fantasy. What would officials make of the empty tomb if and when it was known? How realistic did you find the reported responses of the characters?

Supplemental Stories

With one exception all ten resuscitations in the Bible involved both genders. Look back at the three wrought by Jesus. Notice that they present the three categories of blood relationships within the family: a mother's son, a father's daughter, and the sisters' brother. Prayers of *love* within the family restored *life*. Here are the last five accounts not featured or reviewed above.

Man's Body in Elisha's Grave

Era: Kingdom. Story: 2 Kings 13:20–21. The one exception!
Sometimes bodies of rare people with extraordinary spiritual gifts are credited with supernatural powers. This one stretches my willing suspension of disbelief.

Saints at the Death and Resurrection of Jesus

Era: Incarnation. Story: Matthew 27:50–53.
Is resurrection given not only to the Son of God but also to believers who never met Jesus? Yes, but it's a bit spooky. What were they up to for three days in their tombs?

Peter and Tabitha/Dorcas

Era: Church. Story: Acts 9:36–42.
Peter had witnessed the daughter of Jairus being raised by Jesus. Echoes appear in this account of the power of Christ's presence among this loving church family.

Paul and the Church Family

Era: Church. Story: Acts 14:19–20.
Stoned (with rocks) and dragged through Lystra, Paul lay motionless until the church gathered. How long was it before he took off with Barnabas to the next city?

Eutychus, Paul, and the Church Family

Era: Church. Story: Acts 20:7–12.
Let this be a warning to long-winded preachers in unairconditioned, stuffy church balconies. This account echoes Elijah's and Elisha's action in praying for restored life.

Christ and the Church Resurrected

Era: Eternity. Story: Revelation 19:1–10.
Reread "The Saints' Song" (p. 9) and "The Summary Commission" at the end of Part I (p. 29). Thank you for accepting the invitation to explore God's Grand Story. Alleluia! Amen.

A CLOSER LOOK AT THE
HEARTS OF THE MATTER

Good fiction is believable; good truth changes belief.
—Source unknown

The disciples wondered; they longed; they dreaded. For three days, the souls of the ten who had deserted Jesus in his worst hour were plunged into guilt and grief. Judas had committed suicide. John filled in details of the trials and execution. Likely he had witnessed Peter's denial. When Jesus visited them the evening of the Resurrection, the disciples quaked in fear and trembling. Immediately Jesus offered them peace sealed by the Holy Spirit. Then the disciples heard their assignment, to forgive or retain the sins of others. Jesus knew they could recognize a soul undergoing wrenching remorse, hopeless self-insufficiency, undeserved pardon, and utter devotion born of divine grace. A lot can happen in three days.

We know of no such visitation to the Sadducee Joseph of Arimathea and the Pharisee Nicodemus, who spent a disconsolate sabbath alone. The price exacted of leaders who make life-and-death decisions could hobble and harden their consciences. Dissenters suffered doubly from their failure to convince their colleagues despite their courage in the face of likely censure and expulsion from the Sanhedrin. Before the Holy One of Israel, however, their guilt remained. Their kind and generous treatment of Jesus's body could do no ultimate good because the Law of Moses provided no remedy for the intentional and corporate sin of the Sanhedrin that they had failed to avert. What had they done?! Would history condemn them for killing yet another prophet? What if this man Jesus actually had been the promised Messiah and even the Son of God? If so, what horrors of an angry God would fall upon them and their nation for executing *this* innocent man? They wondered; they longed; they dreaded.

Did they hear news of the empty tomb from one of the bribed Temple guards or one of the chief priests who gave the bribe? No relief there. No one knows how and when undisclosed disciples met the two men. The dynamics crackled with understandable distrust and suspicion. Joseph and Nicodemus conjectured that the disciples really had stolen the body. The disciples feared that the two Sanhedrin members were spying on them for a future arrest and probable crucifixion. Both sides told their stories. An unpredicted disclosure awaited the disciples. Here were two *secret believers from the Sanhedrin* whose conspiracy had obtained Roman permission to torture, mock, and crucify Jesus. Dared the disciples believe the two men? But also, no story before or since offered such an amazing ending than what the Sanhedrin members heard about Resurrection Sunday. Were the religious officials or the apostles more stunned at the revelations at this rendezvous? I do know the Holy Spirit was *not* stunned but strikingly active in this meeting. This interaction presented a crucial test of the apostles' assignment to forgive or to retain sins. Consider their case and that of the two men of the Sanhedrin in silence.

They questioned; they opened their hearts; they confessed their sins; they hoped; and they believed. No one can be convicted of killing someone who enters the courtroom in perfect health to advocate for the accused murderers. Jesus had paid their ransom in his blood and had risen to authenticate rendering their unclean hands spotless. The Judge must declare, "The defendants are ruled 'not guilty.' Case closed," and tap the gavel. Pardoned!

So it came to pass that "The word of God continued to spread; the number of the disciples increased greatly in Jerusalem, and a great many of the priests became obedient to the faith."[1] And "Alleluia! The Lord is risen indeed" still rings from the forgiven around the world.

I hope Joseph and Nicodemus did meet the risen Christ later. They may have heard about Jesus's promise to prepare a place for his followers in his Father's house.[2] Joseph thought, "That's a far better place than the one I prepared for him!" Nicodemus remembered the spices he had given and hoped to hear, "Well done, good and trustworthy slave; … enter into the joy of your master."[3] The Sadducee could no longer deny life after death, and the Pharisee now grasped being "born again" into a new covenant under the law of love.

There is no historical reason for the existence of the Church other than the Resurrection. Without it, the disciples could only mourn a lost cause and head back to fishing, which they did, until the risen Christ commissioned these fishermen to give up their nets to fish for people. It took time to understand what he meant and how to pass on this truth, but they learned with the help of the Holy Spirit.

When Stephen, Peter, Paul, Silas, John, and other apostles soon faced death, imprisonment, and exile for their faith in Jesus, they had no written record from the New Testament and had no idea of the impact the Gospel would have around the world for centuries to come. But they could recall the faithfulness of the LORD of Israel stretching back two millennia. The Hebrew Scriptures they had learned gave them a veritable arsenal of faith: stories to tell, psalms to pray, and prophetic visions to recall. Now they also realized in a new and unexpected way that what the prophets had hoped for, Jesus had delivered.

John had years to meditate on who Jesus was until his old age in exile. Furthermore, as Jesus requested from the cross, Mary moved into his home so he could care for her needs (see p. 47). Until her death, they had hours to share recollections of him. Her insights inevitably influenced John's thinking, especially his themes of *life* and *love* that occur repeatedly in his writings about life as followers of Christ. They connected the LORD of the Hebrew Scriptures with Jesus, Son of God, and discovered deeper understanding of his miraculous signs and teaching embedded in their heritage of faith.[4] They were utterly convinced that the risen Jesus they had seen, heard, and touched and the LORD were One. Jesus's teaching, deeds, death, and Resurrection fired the determination of all the apostles to proclaim good news.

Transcendence, transition, and transfiguration changed the stories that informed their hopes and destinies and those of all who have become sons and daughters of God since then.

CONCLUSION

In most ways, the characters in the Bible differ little from you and me. They were born into a family who gave them a language, habits, and traditions about living together. They observed that people vary in cleverness and speed. They noticed that some people had more and others had less of wealth and health than they had. They learned skills to provide food, clothing, and shelter for their families. They watched the sky for clues about weather. They witnessed the rhythms of seasonal changes. They celebrated occasions of good fortune, nuptials, births, recovery, victory, or increased influence. They pleased all five senses. They experienced disease, war, and death. They wished for relief from pain and hoped to obtain the favor of higher powers. They are we.

They and we can't keep the Ten Commandments. Then come the Great Commandments: Love God with your whole being; love your neighbor as yourself. That overwhelms our circuits. How much is enough to please God? Like Job's wife, why not "Curse God, and die"? For temporary relief, we make gods to feed, please, and appease. But what is the point of all this service of our gods? In the end, we die. Ecclesiastes reiterates, "Vanity of vanities! All is vanity." The best the preacher could do was advise, "Fear God, and keep his commandments; for that is the whole duty of everyone. For God will bring every deed into judgment, including every secret thing, whether good or evil."[1] Without loopholes, the commandments leave us in a limp lump of hopelessness. No exit, so we wonder; we long; and we dread death.

Then Jesus defeated death. The gods tumbled before the Suffering Servant. Love won!

God's Grand Story traces the path of the degrees of love from self-centered love, to grateful love, to awe-filled love, and finally to united love as children of the Triune God. God has constructed various avenues in life that enlarge our opportunities to love. This book has featured stories of the all-encompassing human male and female linkages in the family of origin, sexual encounter(s), and other functional affiliations in the wider community. Each of the three categories involves distinct responsibilities toward one another. They flow from the Triune God's all-encompassing love that offers a true family identity, unconditional mercy to heal guilt and shame, and graceful guidance into a life of good will and service.

The Grand Story came to a climax in the Passion, which revealed the gravity of humankind's deep depravity, and in the Resurrection, which revealed the glory of God's great goodness. The denouement of applied redeeming grace in individuals and groups stretches to this moment, giving life meaning, purpose, and hope. Be assured that while the course of true love never did run smooth, it will be consummated at the perfect time for an eternal marriage.

The Two "Others"

The desire for eternal life depends upon the union of human beings with the eternal Creator of life. Both the God revealed in the pages of the Bible and human beings are *persons who can bond with each other.* Persons exhibit consciousness, words, humor, creativity, intellect, will, and moral accountability exchanged in their communications. Yet no chasm is wider than the holy eternal deity from the imperfect mortal human. We experience the awe-filled brightness and beauty of the holy. We also tremble in the presence of the all-knowing Other who holds access to resonant joy of life and deforming decay of death. We search for peace, ask ultimate questions, and find pointers in nature, ritual, beauty, and sacred literature. These realities impact the arenas of culture, ethnicity, social class, political alignment, language, religion, and law. No person grows to full and true personhood without the God-shaped vacuum in their soul being addressed and peace being sought with the divine Other.

Now attend to these parallels. The desire for earthly life depends upon sexual union for only a man and woman together (or elaborate laboratory imitations) may reproduce the wonder of another human life. Far smaller than the chasm between God and humanity is the difference between the genders. Yet no human difference is more universal and pervasive than gender. Men and women differ physically, emotionally, psychologically, cognitively, sociologically, medically, chemically, and spiritually. Yet God built into human men and women the urge to merge, and sexual activity is "the world's oldest business." Gender also pervades the same lesser arenas as those concerning dealings between God and humanity. No person grows to adulthood without addressing their own and society's expectations in this regard and facing the potential for happiness and strength as well as rejection and alienation.

Both the inherent inclination, denied or affirmed, for the divine "Other" and the gender "other" seek resolution through an intimate bond. The pursuit of this union exposes a person's outlook toward an elemental stranger. My hunch is that dispositions toward God and toward the other gender bear foundational similarities, but I leave you to make your own observations. Stating it negatively, John wrote, "... those who do not love a brother or sister whom they have seen, cannot love God whom they have not seen."[2] At last the word "love" is used about us and our elemental strangers. Solomon shakes his head and wistfully sings his Song of Songs.

In biblically based settings, the two unions of elemental strangers are solemnized in the covenant of Holy Baptism (between Sovereign and servant) and the covenant of holy matrimony (between equals, man and woman). A covenant is a public agreement for terms of peace. It encompasses all of life for all one's life, requires self-limitation of both parties, cannot be purchased, depends upon trustworthy character, seeks divine aid to keep its terms, and, from antiquity, involved bloodshed followed by a shared meal (called "cutting a covenant"). The term "covenant" comes up in many stories in this book and other biblical literature. The marital union is used frequently as a metaphor for the divine–human union. God offered to faithful people two biblical covenants that defined the terms offered by the LORD: the Law-based covenant of the Old Testament (which sadly humans have never kept) and the redemption-based covenant in Christ of the New Testament (which gladly Jesus continues to keep).

In loving commitment to the "Other" and "other" strangers, we may venture into shalom, the peace of God that passes all understanding. As human life comes from the union of man and woman, so spiritual life comes from union with the Triune God. From the imbedded promises exchanged in both covenants waft the fragrance of love from the Triune God.

Other Others

The world we live in is at odds with the purposes of the God revealed in the Bible. Today we see much evidence in many arenas of ill will, pain, and abandonment between men and women. That is a major factor in why this book includes purposefully selected stories in which linked men and women made a difference in God's Grand Story in three contexts: family of origin, sexual encounters, and other functional associations in the wider community. Each chapter included examples along the spectrum of willing obedience to open defiance toward the covenant. Even when the characters acted courageously under God's covenant, they rarely escaped injustice, fear, conflict, or suffering; e.g., Noah and his family, Hannah and Samuel, Jehoiada and Jehoshebeath, Paul and Lydia, and Apollo and Priscilla. When they defied the terms of the covenant, often God graciously gave them a second chance or more to renew the covenant; e.g., Adam and Eve, Moses and Miriam, Samson and Delilah, Ahab and Jezebel, and Peter and the women at the chargrill. With the consent of the characters, sour stories ended better than expected; e.g., Judah and Tamar, Pharaoh and the midwives, Moses and his mother, David and Bathsheba, Haman and Esther, and Jesus and the woman caught in adultery.

The Bible spans nearly two millennia. That's enough time to gather stellar examples of all sorts and conditions of human beings carrying out memorable exploits with each other and God. The unmatched accounts of Jesus show us what constant consonant consent looks like among Father and Son and Spirit. His interactions with women show us what constant consonant consent looks like between the genders. He embodied God's will being done and God's kingdom coming on earth as in heaven.

Torn and Mended

From the beginning, our purpose as men and women, boys and girls, is to reflect the image of God *together*. All of us fall short through self-centeredness, the insecurities of fear, and the list goes on. How easy it is to be hurt by the actions of the other gender! Occasionally something good happens which completely diverts attention away from self and friction with the other gender. Afterward personal forgiveness and mutual reconciliation take place with increasing ease. The Resurrection is the prime example. Chapter 12 (pp. 112–113) of this book describes what *might have happened* between the disciples and the Sanhedrin members, Joseph and Nicodemus. Now, I return to the climax of God's Grand Story to parse out what *really did happen* for peace in the age old "battle of the sexes." It was accomplished though the Passion and completed on Resurrection Day when the victorious King of Kings made his reign certain.

The death of Jesus opened wide the cleavage between the sexes. Without a doubt, exclusively *men* killed Jesus on Good Friday. Judas had arranged the betrayal with leaders of the Sanhedrin, an all-male group. The Sanhedrin drummed up false witnesses (only males permitted) against Jesus which they could not confirm. They charged Jesus with blasphemy, which deserved death in Jewish law. They presented this to the Roman governor, Pilate, by accusing Jesus of being an enemy of Caesar. Pilate decided Jesus was not guilty but handed him over to other men who flogged, taunted, spit upon, and crucified him. Peter denied knowing Jesus to avoid testifying. Terrified, the *men* among the disciples fled.

By contrast, exclusively *women* showed public and private sympathy for Jesus. The most prominent *woman*, Pilate's wife, Claudia, spoke up to her husband in defense of Jesus's innocence to no avail. On the walk to the cross, *women* wept for him, stood by the cross, and followed him to the tomb. Any protest *women* made would have fallen on deaf ears.

But God's orchestration, full of irony and paradox, brought the two genders together to make the Resurrection known. The sign on the cross said Jesus was the King of the Jews. The Roman centurion said Jesus was a son of God. Among the hostile Sanhedrin were two secret believers with the clout to spare his body from desecration and the money to give him a burial fit for royalty. These two steadfastly defied defeat by action of unforeseen momentous impact. The Temple guards sealed up the tomb, but the disciples they thought might steal the body were in hiding. The officials went home thinking the case was closed, with lips sealed. They had no need to revisit that tomb for at least a year when the bones might be stored in an ossuary or by Joseph's own death. Jesus would soon be forgotten. God laughed.

They had ignored the *women* who loved Jesus. Mary Magdalene, Mary mother of James, Joanna, Salome, and other *women* could never have laid claim to the body of Jesus, but they quietly noted the way to the tomb. They prepared for returning after the sabbath to anoint the body with spices that tradition called on *women* to do. (They were used to being unclean regularly anyway.) Alas, the *men* from the Sanhedrin had beaten them to it. Besides, an angel had rolled away the stone and had knocked out the *men* guarding the tomb. Before the guards came to, God's messenger quickly sent off the *women* to tell the hiding disciples that Jesus had risen. Along the way to announce the amazing news, the risen Jesus greeted them in person.

Not unexpectedly the *men* had a hard time believing the *women*'s story, but Peter and John hurried to the tomb to verify their story and believed. Not long after, the officials learned from the awakened guards about the transcendent events that morning at the tomb. They cooked up a self-incriminating story cushioned with a bribe and a promise.

Here's what I don't want you to miss. Had the *men* not saved and buried the body, predatory animals would have devoured much of it, and decay from the hot climate would have left it completely unrecognizable. Had the *women* not visited the tomb, its empty condition would have gone unnoticed and unannounced. Now surely the Almighty could have managed to let the world know of the Resurrection somehow. Over the ages God had used a rainbow in the sky, a talking donkey, and the handwriting on the wall, not to mentions angelic beings, to send messages. But this body belonged to the beloved Son. The Father allowed only kind hands to touch this torn body and lay it to rest. God also knew what we humans needed in order to believe. Mary needed to hear Jesus's voice. The couple going to Emmaus needed to make sense of the kind of Messiah they had not anticipated. Thomas needed to touch the scars. The fishermen needed to watch him cook and eat fish. Peter needed personal assurance that Jesus had work for him to do. All of us need to know he did not come to condemn but to give life and forgiveness. Furthermore, unconnected *men* and *women* who could neither coordinate nor guess the impact of their actions were absolutely necessary peers in the plot who woke up faith and joy that has never gone to sleep. After all, it's *God's* Grand Story, not a human invention.

The Author solemnized and beautified this week of hatred and horror with fragrant bookends of extravagant gifts to Jesus. The first one was applied to his feet and wiped by the hair of a *woman* in Bethany, and the last one was applied throughout the wrapped grave cloths by the hands of a *man* in the tomb. These exquisite details of the Passion perfume the whole of Jesus's supreme gift of self-giving love that will woo the world till the end of time.

The pattern of balance between men and women continues beyond the scope of this book in the symbolism of the book of Revelation. To summarize briefly, a cosmic crime occurs. The Kidnapper has deceived and stolen the children away. A dragon tries to devour the baby a queenly mother is delivering. The archangel Michael and his angels fight the dragon and save the baby and mother. The hero, Son of God and Son of Man, is the only one able to capture and destroy the Kidnapper. Babylon and the Prostitute wage a great battle against the Lamb and the Saints. The Hero pays in blood the ransom demanded. The martyrs of the ages fall on their knees before the mighty throne of God. The Hero reappears as a Lamb that has been killed. The perpetrator of the abysmal crime is thrown into the abyss. Now the kidnapped children can come home. Hear the pipes and piccolos lead the band "when the saints go marchin' in." The victorious Lamb and the Saints celebrate at the celestial wedding with one voice glorifying the God and Father of our Lord Jesus Christ. The story is earthy and awful, but in the end, love wins!

According to the Bible, from beginning to end of human history as we know it, God has paired men and women to fuel a story of love sourced in the Triune God. Thanks to many authors writing over many centuries, a record of this amazing narrative has been carefully treasured and protected by the Almighty in the Old and New Testaments. The pattern of participation of both genders appears regularly throughout God's Grand Story, particularly at crucial pivotal points. The record demonstrates that this is God's intended way of working out large and small details of movement through the four degrees of love that bring us into unity with the two grand elemental strangers: God and the other gender.

We are asked to trust the Lord God of this narrative known to us as the Good Shepherd, the Prince of Peace, the light of the world, the living water and bread of life, the way, the truth, and the Resurrection. Living with faith in God's enduring love and mercy is not only good for an individual but also good for everyone and everything formed by the Creator's hands.

Before You Close the Book

Look back once again at page 31 listing the six songs about the four degrees of love between self and God. Through the Bible stories featured here, we have traced characters on their journeys back and forth within the degrees of love. Despite human vacillations on that course of true love, the Hero never wavers in wooing us. The supreme Other never walked off with what he had not paid for. Jesus returned the borrowed tomb, his grave clothes, and a fortune in spices. The mighty Other does not coerce the beloved human race. The wooing Father and searching Spirit join the Hero in awaiting our response to this query. What is our verdict on letting the Hero who has paid our ransom walk off with us, lock, stock, and barrel?

The Final Puzzler: Perhaps the most frequent and difficult argument against faith goes like this. The God worthy of my worship would make a world in which all was well and people were always perfect. That obviously didn't happen. Therefore, either there is no God or God is not worthy of my devotion. Which of these conditions makes the better and truer story: perpetual human innocence or a grand God ready to redeem human evil for glorious ends?

Now please indulge me by reading the Afterword to learn the source of this book's cover.

AFTERWORD: ROSALIE'S DINER

The list I had begun to compile in 2004 of men and women linked in Bible stories had grown to around 400 entries three years later. Grant LeMarquand, then editor of *Trinity Journal for Theology and Ministry*, expressed interest in publishing an article about this project. After my retirement from school chaplaincy in January, 2008, I continued work on this journal article focusing on biblical examples of the impact of gender in spiritual formation and deformation. Then an unwelcome intrusion confirmed the timing of my retirement and an imminent move from DC suburbs to my tiny getaway place on Lake Erie.

On Monday morning, January 28, 2008, Dennis Jacob, my brother-in-law, was shoveling snow when he noticed that his neck was swelling. He had already made an appointment for Tuesday with his family doctor, about a protrusion in his abdomen that my sister Rachel had noticed. Nevertheless, she hurried Dennis to the ER nearest their home in Mercer, Pennsylvania. Late that afternoon, my phone rang. Dennis had a large mass in his lower abdomen with lymphoma the suspected cause. After the Tuesday appointment with the family doctor, she immediately referred him to oncologist Dr. George Garrow for a biopsy of the tumor.

When the biopsy showed non-Hodgkin's B-cell lymphoma, Denny began a series of six to eight chemo treatments. Rachel and Dennis could tell that the abdominal mass was shrinking. Their daughter Tabitha traveled to be with her dad two days a week, and she shaved his head when his hair began to fall out. Her best friend, Nadia, collected sponsors and completed a triathlon near Alcatraz prison to raise funds for lymphoma research. Tabitha began to run, too. Their pastor and a church elder who had had cancer anointed him with oil and prayed with him. Piles of cards poured in from friends, neighbors, and churches. Help came in too many ways to list. One example still puts Rachel in tears. Nurses recommended a drink that patients had found helpful, and the producers were offering a $5 coupon. Friends loaded her mailbox with so many coupons that the pharmacy had to order a larger supply.

They drenched their 37th anniversary on March 20 with tears. Dennis had not enough strength to pick up a spring bouquet of flowers and chocolate-coated pretzels for Rachel. Malignant pleural effusion, a life-threatening fluid accumulating between the outer layers of Denny's lungs, had been drained from his chest cavity earlier. A second draining had to be done on their anniversary. In the spring we cheered from the windows as Denny attempted to mow the lawn, but he still struggled to breathe. The medication for pleural effusion was not working.

In early summer, Dr. Garrow told them Denny had follicular non-Hodgkin's lymphoma. A second opinion from the leading oncologist in Pittsburgh confirmed the diagnosis. Because of his cold recital of the prognosis, they dubbed him Dr. Death. The slow-growing small-cell follicular non-Hodgkin's lymphoma, which he may have had for years, had defused into aggressive large B-cell lymphoma. Dennis had a 50-50 chance of living two to five years, and if he lived longer, a 30 percent chance of dying within ten years. Characteristically the defused disease presents multiple relapses until all options are exhausted. Dr. Death recommended periodic PET scans to monitor the disease. This was not going away; it was *incurable*. The grim prognosis delivered a second blow. "Tell Jesus that!" I retorted angrily when I heard the dreadful prediction.

Rachel's methodical schedule and organized division of labor kept their home beautiful. They made a list of what he needed to teach her about the chores he did. She had never even had to fill their cars' gas tanks. Denny's identical twin brother wept, and I was devastated, to observe the contrast between Kenny's healthy physique and Denny's gaunt frame and gray skin. He was dying before our eyes. Kenny and his wife, Karen, visited regularly bearing appetizing comfort food. After six chemo sessions, the doctor decided to stop treatments to see how the cancer would react. Rachel walked a lonely tightrope between what the doctors and her research told her and what might keep hope alive for Dennis, who did not want to hear details. Only a wise wife who knows her husband's heart intimately and loves him deeply could accomplish that.

Clouds were gathering over Dennis, and he barely clung to faith as darkness seeped into his spirit. In an attempt to feel normal again, a.k.a. denial, Denny decided to go back to work as soon as he recovered from the last treatment. In mid-August, he made a lunch appointment with one of his customers, David Meeker, at their habitual lunch venue, Rosalie's Diner in Strasburg, Ohio. The two Christian men took a table in a back room away from the busy tables and counter. During lunch, an elderly woman approached them. She had happened to stop by and had been asked to pray for a man in the back room. Denny's appearance was a dead giveaway for who needed prayer. He gave her permission, pushed aside his lunch, and laid his head on his folded arms. She gently rubbed his bald head, put her hands on his bony, thin shoulders, and prayed. He felt a ring of warmth move slowly from his head to his toes. The woman left.

Denny said nothing about this for several days and then mentioned the puzzling request and sensation to Rachel. On Friday, September 5, I visited them. During our conversation, Denny asked what I thought of a strange event that had happened on a sales call. Suspecting that the whole event reeked with the power of suggestion, I blurted out like a fool, "Denny, did you know that people who are being healed often feel a current of warmth?" Surprised, he answered, "No. Really?" I kicked myself for raising Rachel's and his hopes.

The following Tuesday, he packed his suitcase for a week in the hospital for surgical procedures. One lung had collapsed by 80 percent and the other by 40 percent. A tiny camera would be inserted into his chest cavity to try to find the blockage, and locate and seal the leak causing pleural effusion. Before the procedure, they took another X-ray. Are you sitting down? His lungs were normal; the fluid was gone; his sense of smell had returned; and no scar tissue showed. The last discovery removed the need for corrective surgery from the period of time his lungs had been partially collapsed. After the astounded couple left the hospital free to go home, the doctor monitoring and treating the pleural effusion called Denny's oncologist and literally yelled into the phone, referring to Denny's last name, "Pull up Jacob's X-rays! Have you seen the X-rays?" The rattled Dr. Garrow could barely hit the right keys on the computer and said, "Just tell me the results." The prudent oncologist was non-committal, but his intern was thrilled at the unexpected results and the story of the woman's prayer. When the family doctor heard about it, she was open to the healing power of prayer, and he did begin to regain strength. Thanks to Dr. Death's recommended PET scans, the scan early in 2009 came back showing NED (no evidence of disease). The news came the day before Dennis attended his father's funeral. "We have this treasure in clay jars, so that it may be made clear that this extraordinary power belongs to God and does not come from us ... For while we live, we are always being given up to death for Jesus' sake, so that the life of Jesus may be made visible in our mortal flesh."[1] Dr. Death was stunned; the lymphoma has never recurred.

Denny and Rachel celebrated recently their 50th wedding anniversary. They treasure three mementos. The first was a hand-drawn get-well card from a little girl that they tucked inside her high school graduation gift. A woman had composed and recorded in her journal a prayer during his illness and sent it to him years afterward. (Rereading journals is a spiritual discipline not to be neglected.) But Denny really loves to show off a joyous photo of Tabitha and him. Their hands are clasped in the air as they cross the finish line at his first half marathon at age 65.

Now here is the backstory. David Meeker lunched regularly at Rosalie's Diner and had told the waitresses of Denny's grave illness. Several months into Denny's remarkable recovery, the two men again had lunch at Rosalie's Diner. Once again, the 83-year-old woman just happened to stop by, and Denny learned her story. Evelyn Anslow's husband had pastored a nearby church and augmented his preaching from a tent during the summer months. After his death, she continued his ministry with the help of their son. At that time, she had offered to the diner's owner to bake pies and peel potatoes for free if he would allow her to pray for patrons who desired it. He agreed, and she came in two days a week. One day when she stopped in unexpectedly, a waitress asked her to please go to the back room and pray for a jovial customer who looked terrible now. When Denny told Evelyn what had happened since she prayed for him, she wept with joy and gratitude to God. The waitresses gathered around to hear of the healing that began in their humble diner. Denny has had many other opportunities to tell this story of God's life-transforming mercy.

In 2009, my article about connections between men and women that made a formative difference in God's story was published. A couple of professors encouraged me to develop the list into a book. I was doubtful because I had come out of retirement to serve as a hospice chaplain and then in one last parish commitment. Writing a book would demand long, hard work, expose my thoughts to a rarely receptive public, and make little to no money. If it happened at all, it would have to wait until my next retirement.

As I prayed about this matter, I was struck by undercurrents of bonded men and women in Denny's story: three hardworking and devoted husbands and wives, a father and a daughter, a mother and a son in ministry, an owner of a diner and an unpaid, praying, pie-producing potato peeler (try saying that quickly), a waitress who recognized Denny's need, another waitress grieving the loss of her brother and husband to follicular lymphoma, a woman raising funds for her friend's father, another woman writing down a prayer for Dennis, a woman physician and men in medical specialties, caring nurses who looked forward to visits from a patient with an incurable cancer and an even more incurable sense of humor, and, yes, this sister-in-law and her ever helpful brother-in-law.

It occurred to me that every man and woman, boy and girl, in this story lived the answer to their prayer, "Thy kingdom come, Thy will be done on earth as in heaven." The miracles Jesus performed gave the witnesses a glimpse of his Father's will and kingdom. The miracle at Rosalie's Diner involved many who were faithful to God's covenant, exercised their particular gifts and callings as citizens of God's realm, and acted as one united family of God's children. I envisioned many kinds of healing we might see in our out-of-whack times if people absorbed wisdom from biblical case studies of men, women, and God. So I started to plan an adult Bible story book for you. None of us knows when, but before long, we may find ourselves laughing together in holy hilarity and weeping together in joy and gratitude.

Do you feel a tap on your shoulder to join a cloud of partners in the dance with the Triune God who woos the world?

ACKNOWLEDGEMENTS

It all began with my parents' Christmas gift of a black zippered, red-letter King James Version with my name engraved on the front cover when I was five years old *and* two sisters, Miriam "Mim" Chapman and Rachel Jacob, who keep challenging me to examine faith to this day. I owe a debt of gratitude to scores of companions in thousands of small group Bible studies over the past sixty years, dozens of teachers, preachers, and seminary professors, hundreds of students from age two to the nineties, and, above all, the Triune God who made all this possible.

Three churches opened doors to generate this book. First, Rector Billy M. Shand, III, and school board chairman, Gary Bachman, at St. Francis Episcopal Church in Potomac, MD, called me to be the chaplain of the parish day school where I had the rare privilege of teaching Bible stories full time for a decade (1998–2008). Second, after serving (2011–17) on the pastoral staff with Rector Donald Binder at the historic Pohick Episcopal Church in Lorton, VA, the parishioners gave a generous retirement gift which amply covered the costs of producing this book. Third, two choir members at All Saints Episcopal Church in Chevy Chase, MD, gave invaluable help. Longtime friend, Lisbeth Bagnold, gave a kick-start gift to begin and then put me in contact with a patient and skilled editor, Fiona Little, to finish the project.

Two professors, Les Fairfield and James C. Wilhoit, encouraged me to continue exploring biblical narratives for adult readers. During the planning stages of this book, a handful of biblical scholars critiqued a premise based upon the accounts of the origin and purpose of gender in the early chapters of Genesis. Thank you to J. Richard Middleton, John H. Walton, Richard Clouser, and Bea Dorsey for personal conversations, responses to my questions about Hebrew culture and language, and referrals to useful resources.

Endurance awards go to noteworthy fellow pilgrims. Roman and Arlene Cybak frequently opened their spare bedrooms for writing retreats. Margie and Paul Coran and Lucinda A. Kolpien painstakingly checked biblical references. Helpful conversations with Diana Campbell, Tony Giglio, Eileen Kasmierowiz, David G. O'Connor, and Carolyn Lincoln influenced the approach, title, and content. Linda Eller double checked galley corrections with me. Spiritual director Claire-Lise Kelly listened and offered wisdom throughout the years of contemplating and completing the writing process.

Finally, the dozen or so clergy who have met weekly to study the Bible for well over a decade at Greenspring in Springfield, VA, have provided a spiritual home thoroughly anchored in God's reign and will on earth here and now as in heaven. I treasure their grace and weathered experience in applying biblical concepts in all circumstances with all sorts and conditions of people, kind of like the characters we meet in Bible stories.

APPENDIX A: PARALLEL STORIES OF MEN AND WOMEN

Appendix A represents discoveries noted over many readings of Scripture, and more are likely to be uncovered. The four lists in Appendix A are not exhaustive while Appendices B–D list every example in the category.

1. Proximate Doublet Accounts

In these examples, similar stories about each gender are placed in proximity to each other. The increase of instances in the New Testament may reflect awareness of the Holy Spirit's formation of the church family in which both genders are to enjoy attentive recognition. There are probably more examples to be found.

Exodus 15:1–21: Moses & Miriam: songs after deliverance from Pharaoh

Judges 13: Manoah & wife: angel visits each about Samson

Nehemiah, Esther: Nehemiah & Esther: two sacrificial leaders

Matthew 8:5–17: Centurion's servant & Peter's mother-in-law: healed to serve

Matthew 9:18–31: Blind men & ill women: healing two of each gender

Matthew 13:31–33, Luke 13:18–21: Man's mustard seed & woman's leaven: parables of God's hidden kingdom

Matthew 24:40, Luke 17:35–36 (some translations omit verse 36): Two field workers (men) & grain grinders (women): one taken and one left behind

Matthew 25:1–30: Servants' talents & ten bridesmaids: parables of preparedness

Matthew 27:57–66, Mark 15:40–16:2, Luke 23:50–24:1, John 19:38–20:2: Joseph, Nicodemus & women at burial of Jesus: preparation of spices.

Mark 5:1–34, Luke 8:26–48: Gerasene demoniac & hemorrhaging woman: cure of long illness

Mark 7:24–37: Deaf/mute man & Greek woman: healing outside Jewish territory

Luke 2:25–38: Simeon & Anna: Temple greeters for baby Jesus's family

Luke 7:1–17: Centurion's servant & widow in Nain: loved one's health restored

Luke 15:1–10: Shepherd's sheep & woman's coin: parables of lost and found

Luke 18:1–14: Tax collector & widow: parables of effective prayers

Luke 20:45—21:4: Proud scribes & poor widow: exploitative and sacrificial motives

John 3:1–21, 4:1–42: Nicodemus & woman at Sychar: Notable conversations with Jesus

John 4: Official's son & Samaritan woman: non-Jews Jesus healed

Acts 9:32–43: Aeneas & Dorcas: healed in ministry of Peter

Acts 16:13–40: Jailer & Lydia: hospitality in Philippi

1 Thessalonians 2:7, 11: Father & mother: similes used by Paul about himself

Hebrews 11:8–12: Abraham & Sarah: faith exercised in great uncertainty

James 2:20–26: Abraham & Rabab: faith counted as righteousness

2. Stories of Men and Women Mirrored in the Old and New Testaments

These paired stories show continuity in how God works with individuals regardless of gender and era, Old Testament (OT) or New Testament (NT). Human character and concerns also stretch across millennia for some of these types of events still occur today.

Initial members of a new community:
OT Adam & Eve, Old Covenant: Genesis 1–3, based on obedience
NT Joseph & Mary, New Covenant: Matthew 1, Luke 2, based on grace

Woman from man's body, man from woman's body:
OT Eve from Adam: Genesis 2
NT Jesus from Mary: Luke 1–2

Woman's seed to crush Satan's head:
OT The woman (Eve): Genesis 3:15
NT The Church as bride of Christ: Romans 16:17–20

Runaway slaves who returned and were restored temporarily to their owners:
OT Hagar to Sarah and Abraham: Genesis 16
NT Onesimus to Philemon: Philemon

At a source of life-giving water, non-Jewish women in troubled relationships with men were first to encounter the revelation of deity in person:
OT Angel & Hagar: Genesis 16:7–14, theophany at a spring
NT Jesus & woman at Sychar: John 4:25–26, Messiah at Jacob's well

Met the God who sees:
OT Hagar: Genesis 16:13–15
NT Nathaniel: John 1:45–50

Short-sighted decisions without remedy:
OT Esau: Genesis 25:29–34, 27:1–45
NT Foolish bridesmaids: Matthew 25:1–13

Manipulators for gain who lost what they gained:
OT Rebekah lost Jacob who fled after deception for blessing: Genesis 25:28, 27:1—28:5
NT Judas betrayed Jesus for 30 pieces of silver, returned it, committed suicide: Matthew 26:14–16, 47–50, 27:3–10; Mark 14:10–11, 43–50; Luke 22:3–6, 47–48; John 12:4–8, 13:18–30, 18:2–3, Acts 1:15–22

Two significant sets of siblings, 2 brothers with 1 sister, 2 sisters with 1 brother:
OT Miriam, Aaron, Moses: Exodus 2:1–10, 4:10–16; Numbers 26:59
NT Lazarus, Martha, Mary: John 11

Declaration that this faithful group is to be a priestly kingdom and holy nation:
OT Moses to Israel: Exodus 19:6
NT Peter to Church: 1 Peter 2:5b–9

Role reversal in supply of spices and cloth:
OT Men — spices, women — cloth: Exodus 35:25–29
NT Men — cloth, women — spices: Matthew 27:59, Mark 16:1–3, Luke 23:53–56, John 19:40

Sons-in-law instrumental in recovery of mothers-in-law:
OT Boaz & Naomi: Ruth 2–4
NT Peter & his wife's mother: Matthew 8:14–15, Mark 1:29–31, Luke 4:38–39

Outstanding leaders from long-barren mothers:
OT Samuel & Hannah: 1 Samuel 1–2
NT John the Baptist & Elizabeth: Luke 1

Worshipful prayers of women about their sons:
OT Hannah: 1 Samuel 2:1–10
NT Mary's *Magnificat*: Luke 1:46–55

Anointing of a king:
OT Samuel anointed David: 1 Samuel 16
NT Mary of Bethany anointed Jesus: John 12:1–8

Manipulators for another person's death:
OT Saul required 100 foreskins, hoping David would be killed: 1 Samuel 17:5, 18.5–29, 25:44; 2 Samuel 3:12–16
NT Herodias's daughter tricked Herod for John the Baptist's head: Matthew 14:3–12, Mark 6:17–29

Men reprimanded for their treatment of women:
OT Nathan, David & Bathsheba: 2 Samuel 12
NT Jesus, Simon & unwelcome woman at dinner: Mark 14:3–9

Foreigners seeking wisdom:
OT Solomon & Queen of Sheba: 1 Kings 10:1–13: 2 Chronicles 9:1–12 (Luke 11:31)
NT Philip & Eunuch of Candace: Acts 8:26–40

Women received back a son or brother from almost certain death:
OT Moses & Jochebed, Miriam: Exodus 1:15–2:10, by Pharaoh's decrees
OT Son & widow of Zarephath: 1 Kings 17:7–24
OT Son & Shunammite mother: 2 Kings 4:8–37
NT Son & widow of Nain: Luke 7:11–16
NT Lazarus & Martha, Mary: John 11

Poor widows offered all they had to God's representatives:
OT Widow of Zarephath to Elijah: 1 Kings 17:7–16
NT Widow's mites to temple: Mark 12:41–44, Luke 21:1–4

Gentile women pled for a son or a daughter:
OT Son & widow of Zarephath: 1 Kings 17:17–24 (Elijah)
NT Daughter of Canaanite woman: Matthew 15:21–28, Mark 7:24–30 (Jesus)

Foreigners sought healing for sons:
OT Widow of Zarephath: 1 Kings 17:17–24 (Elijah)
NT Royal official: John 4:46–54 (Jesus)

Parent sought help for dying child of the other gender:
OT Shunammite woman for son: 2 Kings 4:8–37
NT Synagogue ruler for daughter: Matthew 9:18–26, Mark 5:21–43, Luke 8:40–56

Women messengers to men restored faithful fellowship:
OT Huldah to Josiah's officials: 2 Kings 22:11–20
NT Mary Magdalene, other women to disciples: Matthew 28:5–8, Mark 16:6–8, Luke 24:6–10

Made way for a greater deliverer to come:
OT Vashti to Esther: Esther 1
NT John the Baptist to Jesus: Isaiah 40:3–5; Matthew 3:3, Mark 1:2–4, Luke 1, 3:2–6, John 1:19–27

Men unwisely ignored wife's advice:
OT Haman & Zeresh: Esther 6:12–14
NT Pilate & wife [Claudia]: Matthew 27:19

Trio of highest official with a blood-related man and woman upheld justice in unity:
OT Ahasuerus, Mordecai & Esther: Esther 8, 9:29—10:3
NT Festus, Agrippa II & Bernice: Acts 26:30–32

***Disloyal* members with common bonds between each other**:
OT Job & *his wife*: Job 2:9–10
NT *Judas* & Mary of Bethany: John 12:1–8

Special recognition to the daughters of spiritual leaders:
OT Job's three beautiful daughters: Job 42:13–15
NT Philip's four prophet daughters: Acts 21:8–9

Called to be God's prophet in their mothers' wombs:
OT Isaiah, Jeremiah: Isaiah 49:1, 5; Jeremiah 1:4–5
NT John the Baptist: Luke 1:8–17, 39–45

Prophetic visions of one gender protecting the other gender:
OT Women surround men: Jeremiah 31:22
NT Archangel Michael avenges woman attacked by dragon: Revelation 12

Both genders to prophesy and have visions:
OT Joel's prophetic word: Joel 2:28–32
NT Peter's quote at Pentecost: Acts 2:17–21

3. Mirrored Traits, Tasks, Toxins, and Tonics

Biblical narratives portray both men (M) and women (W) with honorable and dishonorable character traits. A given character trait does not belong naturally to a particular gender. Nor do the narratives prescribe certain work for men only or for women only.[1]

Miracle birth sons later were restored to life:
M Abraham, Isaac: Genesis 21:1–7, 22:1–19
W Shunammite woman: 2 Kings 4:18–37

Generously watered sheep/camels for other gender:
W Rebekah for Abraham's servant: Genesis 24:17–23, 42–47 (camels)
M Moses for Jethro's 7 daughters: Exodus 2:15b–22 (sheep)

Tenacity for divine aid:
M Jacob: Genesis 32:22–32
W Shunammite woman: 2 Kings 4:30

Accepted pain for greater good, "If I am bereaved/perish, I am bereaved/perish ...":
M Jacob for sons: Genesis 43:14c
W Esther for her people: Esther 4:16

Great deliverers:
M Moses: Pentateuch (Genesis–Deuteronomy)
W Esther: Esther

Instrumental in killing a member of the other gender in a political conflict:
W Jael killed Commander Sisera: Judges 4:11–24
W Delilah trapped Samson: Judges 16:15–31
M Benjaminites at Gibeah killed a concubine from Bethlehem: Judges 19:16–30
M Eunuchs killed Queen Jezebel at command of Joab: 2 Kings 9:30–37

Kinsmen redeemers:
M Boaz for Ruth: Ruth
W Esther for Mordecai and Jews: Esther

Crucial choices, made / turned down:
W Move to Bethlehem: Ruth / Orpah: Ruth 1
M Levirate marriage by next-of-kin: Boaz / closer next-of-kin: Ruth 4

Royalty who ordered their subjects to murder someone who got in their way:
M David, to get rid of Uriah: 2 Samuel 11–12
W Jezebel, to get rid of Naboth: 1 Kings 21

Murderous father with murderous son and murderous mother with murderous daughter:
M David and Absalom: 2 Samuel 11:14–17, 13:28–29
W Jezebel and Athaliah: 1 Kings 18:1–6; 2 Kings 11:1; 2 Chronicles 22:10

Servant girls who conveyed important messages to men:
M Hushai to David via girl: 2 Samuel 17:17
W Naaman to king via maidservant of Naaman's wife: 2 Kings 5:2–4

Captured in war but offered captors helpful advice:
W Naaman's servant girl for healing: 2 Kings 5
M Daniel's dream interpretations: Daniel 2, 4, 5

Focal characters in the birth narratives about Jesus:
M Joseph and Herod: Matthew 1–2
W Elizabeth and Mary: Luke 1–2

Gentiles Jesus healed long distance at request of someone who cared about them:
M Centurion for a servant: Matthew 8:5–13, Luke 7:1–10
W Canaanite woman for daughter: Matthew 15:21–28, Mark 7:24–30

Sins forgiven by Jesus:
M Paralytic: Matthew 9:1–8, Mark 2:1–12, Luke 5:17–26
W Guest with ointment: Luke 7:36–50

Children of leaders healed by Jesus:
W Ruler of synagogue's daughter: Matthew 9:18–26, Mark 5:21–43, Luke 8:40–56
M Royal official's son: John 4:46–54

People Jesus described by calling them animals:
W Canaanite woman, pet dog: Matthew 15:15–28, Mark 7:24–30
M Herod, fox: Luke 13:32

Children healed by Jesus at request of same-gender parent:
W Syrophoenician/Canaanite girl: Matthew 15:21–28, Mark 7:24–30
M Epileptic boy: Matthew 17:14–18, Mark 9:14–27, Luke 9:37–43

Outcasts welcomed by Jesus:
M Tax collectors: Matthew 21:31–32
W Prostitutes: Matthew 21:31–32

Instructed to go to Galilee after Jesus's Resurrection:
M Jesus to disciples before his death: Matthew 26:32, Mark 14:28
W Angel to women after his death: Matthew 28:7, Mark 16:7

Gave warning that was ignored followed by three failures on Good Friday:
W [Claudia] warned husband, Pilate: Matthew 27:19, Luke 23:14, 20, 22

M Jesus warned Peter of 3 denials: Matthew 26:33–35, 69–75, Mark 14:29–31, 66–72, Luke 22:31–34, 54–62, John 13:36–38, 18:17–18, 25–27

Offspring whom Jesus resuscitated:
W Daughter of Jairus: Matthew 9:18–26, Mark 5:21–43, Luke 8:40–56
M Son of widow from Nain: Luke 7:11–16

The risen Jesus chided men for not believing the women's report of resurrection:
M disciples: Mark 16:11, 14
W Mary Magdalene, Joanna, Mary mother of James, et al.: Luke 24:10–11

Prophecy about John the Baptist's purpose regarding Jesus:
M Zechariah: Luke 1:5–23
W Elizabeth: Luke 1:39–45

Forerunners who confirmed identity of a greater person:
W Elizabeth for Mary: Luke 1:36–45
M John the Baptist for Jesus: John 1:24–42

Knew the Redeemer had come:
M Simeon: Luke 2:25–35
W Anna: Luke 2:36–38

Gentiles healed by God's grace in the Old Testament cited by Jesus:
W Widow of Zarephath: Luke 4:24–26
M Naaman: Luke 4:27

Jesus criticized for healing on the Sabbath:
M Withered hand: Luke 6:6–10
W Bent-over woman unable to stand straight upright: Luke 13:10–17

Jesus defended his healing on the Sabbath with the same retort:
W Bent-over woman: In Luke 13.10–17, verse 15
M Dropsy: In Luke 14.1–6, verse 5

Jesus called them children of Abraham:
W Bent-over woman: Luke 13:16
M Zaccheus: Luke 19:9

First appearances of the risen Christ:
W Mary Magdalene: John 20:11–18
M Peter, later on that day before Christ went to Emmaus: Luke 24:34

Jesus knew them before meeting them:
M Nathanael: John 1:43–51
W Woman at Sychar: John 4:17–18

Men not convinced of a woman's report about Jesus until Jesus authenticated it:
W Woman at Sychar: John 4:28–29
M Samaritans of Sychar: John 4:39–42
W Mary Magdalene et al.: Luke 24:8–12
M Disciples: Luke 24:36–52

Fragrant gifts given at beginning and end of Jesus' Passion:
W Mary of Bethany: John 12:1–8
M Nicodemus: John 19:38–42

In John's account, the first verbal responses to the risen Christ confirmed that they belonged to the same Father and God:[2]
W Mary Magdalene: John 20:17–18
M Thomas: John 20:28–29

Greed-driven incidences with supernatural witchcraft:
M Simon the Sorcerer: Acts 8:9–25
W Slave-girl fortune teller: Acts 16:16–21

First Greek converts in Athens:
M Dionysius: Acts 17:34
W Demaris: Acts 17:34

People in conflict addressed by Paul:
W Euodia and Syntyche: Philippians 4:2–3
M Hymenaeus and Alexander: 1 Timothy 1:18–20

Chose to identify with God's people by faith:
M Moses: Hebrews 11:24–27, 31
W Rahab: James 2:25

Addressees of letters written by John:
W The elect lady (a certain woman or figuratively the Church as bride of Christ): 2 John 1
M Gaius, elder in church: 3 John 1

4. Unified Men and Women Acting Together

In these stories, the texts specifically mention men and women taking part together in crucial pivotal events. Order here is roughly chronological.

Genesis 3:6–10, 21
The naked Adam and Eve (Everyman and Everywoman) received grace together when God covered them with garments of skin.

Genesis 17:4–5, 15–16
God gave both Abram and Sarai new names when they entered the covenant with the LORD. Together they would pass the covenant down the generations of their descendants.

Exodus 11:2–3
Men and women among the Hebrews obediently gathered articles of silver and gold given to them by their neighbors.

Deuteronomy 31:9–13
Every seven years, Moses called for all the people to hear the Law read and to learn to honor God.

Joshua 8:30–35
Joshua read the entire Law of Moses to the entire community including all men, women, and children.

2 Kings 23:1–3
Josiah's reforms began after he himself stood in the Temple to read the Law to all the inhabitants, and they agreed to the covenant.

Matthew 1:18—2:23, Luke 1:26–38
To protect and give Jesus a family, Mary and Joseph, individually and together, accepted and followed what God told them.

Luke 1:5–25, 57–80
Together Zechariah and Elizabeth agreed in the company of their neighbors that their son, named John, would turn people to God.

Luke 2:25–38
Simeon and Anna, who spent many hours at the Temple, recognized baby Jesus as the Messiah and spread the word.

Matthew 21:31–32
Jesus sought out outcasts like the tax collectors (men) and prostitutes (women).

Mark 5:25–29, 6:53–56

Woman believed she would be healed if she touched Jesus's garments, and many more people were healed who did the same. See also Matthew 9:20–21, 14:34–36.

Luke 10:1–24 (see also 1 Corinthians 9:5)

Jesus sent out 70 pairs, some of them married, to communities in the region to prepare the people for his visit to come.

John 4:27–29, 39–43

The Samaritans at Sychar believed after hearing what both the woman at the well and Jesus told them.

Matthew 19:29, Mark 10:9–30, Luke 18:29b–30; 1 Corinthians 7

In Matthew's and Mark's Gospels, no blood relationship was to take priority over the kingdom of God, but Luke included spouses also in his list of secondary relationships. Paul's view of marriage (in a context of active persecution) placed the kingdom first.

Luke 24:50–53; Acts 1:1–14, 2:1–18

Jesus blessed his disciples, men and women, who continued to praise and pray in the Temple together while they waited for the Holy Spirit to be manifested.

Acts 9:1–2, 22:4–5

The growth of the early church threatened Saul/Paul's beliefs, so he obtained papers to have both men and women imprisoned for following "the Way" of Christ.

Acts 10:47, 16:15, 32

When the key man or woman in a household converted to follow Jesus Christ, the whole household was baptized as a family together as Cornelius, Lydia, and the Philippian jailer did.

Acts 13:44–52

The united opposition from Jewish "devout women of high standing and the leading men of the city" led Paul to evangelize Gentiles, who received the Gospel joyfully.

Acts 15:1–35; 1 Corinthians 6:9–20; 1 Thessalonians 4:3–8

Differences between Jewish and Gentile believers caused disunity. After close listening, the church leaders decided upon prohibitions against foods unacceptable to Jews and requirements of honorable relationships among unmarried men and women.

Acts 17:1–15

In Thessalonica and Beroea, Paul, Silas, and Timothy found many receptive Jews and devout Greek women and men of high standing ready to study and accept that Jesus was the Messiah.

Acts 18:1–11, 24–28

Church leaders in Corinth were from Corinth (Crispus), Jerusalem (Silas, Paul), Rome (Priscilla, Aquila), and Alexandria (Apollos), and included those with dual Jewish-Greek heritages (Timothy) and devout Greeks (Titius Justus), teaching and learning in unity regardless of gender and nationality. See Appendix C.

Revelation 5:9–14, 7:9–12

Ransomed "saints from every tribe and language and people and nation" are made into "a kingdom and priests serving our God" to join with all the creatures on and under earth and in the sea to give the Lamb honor and glory forever and ever.

APPENDIX B: WOMEN IN THE LIFE OF JESUS

Jesus immortalized a greater number of women and their stories than anyone in history, and *in every case*, for their laudable faith and devotion. This appendix lists all the interactions of Jesus with women recorded in the Gospels. Note that some women are not named, others are not identified the same way in the four Gospels, and groups could be a handful to over a dozen.

Mt = Matthew; Mk = Mark; Lk= Luke; Jn = John, abbreviated after first citation in an entry.
References separated by a comma refer to the same incident in another Gospel.
References separated by // refer to different incidents.
Italicized = more than one unnamed woman in a group.
Underlined = women at the cross.
[--] = information not identified in the Bible but from extra-biblical sources.

(1) Mary, his mother: Matthew 1:18–2.23 // Luke 1:26–2.52 // Mt 12:46–50, Mark 3:31–35, Lk 8:19–21 // Mt 13:55, Mk 6:3 // John 2:1–11 // Jn 6:42 // Jn 19:25–27 // Acts 1:14 // Revelation 12:1–6 (symbolic)

(2) Elizabeth with prenatal Jesus: Luke 1:39–45

(3) Anna with baby Jesus: Luke 2:36–38

(4) Cana bride: John 2:1–11

(5) Peter's mother-in-law: Matthew 8:14–17, Mark 1:29–31, Luke 4:38–39

(6) Wife of Peter/Cephas (wife not directly noted in the Gospels): 1 Corinthians 9:5

(7) Widow of Nain: Luke 7:11–17

(8) "Sinful woman" at Simon's home in Galilee: Luke 7:36–50 [possibly same person as #9]

(9) Mary Magdalene: Luke 8:1–3 [possibly same person as #8]
Matthew 27:56, 61, Mark 15:40–41, 47 // Mt 28:1, Mk 16:1, 9, Lk 24:10 // John 19:25–29 // Jn 20:1–2, 11–18

(10) Joanna: Luke 8:1–3 // Lk 24:10

(11) Susanna: Luke 8:1–3.

(12) Synagogue ruler's daughter: Matthew 9:18–26, Mark 5:21–43, Luke 8:40–56

(13) Jairus's wife: Mark 5:21–43, Luke 8:40–56

(14) Hemorrhaging woman: Matthew 9:20–22, Mark 5:25–34, Luke 8:43–48

(15) *Jesus's sisters*: Matthew 13:55, Mark 6:3

(16) Canaanite/Syrophoenician woman: Matthew 15:21–28, Mark 7:24–30

(17) *Women in 35 pairs sent out*: Luke 10:1–20

(18) Woman at the well at Sychar: John 4:4–42

(19) Woman caught in adultery: John 8:2–11

(20) Mary of Bethany: Luke 10:38–42 // John 11:1–48 // Jn 12:1–8 // Matthew 26:6–13, Mark 14:3–9 [possibly same person as #21]

(21) Woman with perfume: Matthew 26:6–13, Mark 14:3–9 [possibly same person as #20] // Luke 7:36–50

(22) Martha of Bethany: Luke 10:38–42 // John 11:1–48 // Jn 12:2

(23) Woman blessing Jesus's mother: Luke 11:27–28

(24) Bent-over woman: Luke 13:10–17

(25) *Mothers of children blessed*: Matthew 19:13–15, Mark 10:13–16, Luke 18:15–17

(26) Widow with two mites: Mark 12:41–44, Luke 21:1–4

(27) *Peter's denial of Jesus to maid(s) of the high priest while Jesus was being questioned*: Matthew 26:58, 69–75, Mark 14:54, 66–72, Luke 22:54–62 especially verse 61, John 18:15–18, 25–27

(28) <u>*Daughters of Jerusalem*</u>: Luke 23:27–31

(29) Pilate's wife [Claudia]: Matthew 27:19

(30) <u>The other Mary, mother of Joses and James, the younger</u>: Matthew 27:56, 61, Mark 15:40–41, 47 // Mt 28:1, Mk 16:1, Luke 24:10 [possibly same person as #31 and/or #32]

(31) <u>Mary, wife of Clopas/Cleophas (King James Version)</u>: John 19:25 [possibly same person as #30 and/ or #32]
[Joseph's brother, Mary's brother-in-law, Jesus's uncle, 2C Hegesippus][3]

[Clopas and Alphaeus are the same name in Aramaic.][4]

(32) <u>Mary's sister [-in-law?]</u>: John 19:5 [possibly same person as #30 and/or #31]

(33) <u>Salome, mother of James and John of Zebedee</u>: Matthew 20:20–28, Mark 10:35–45 // Mt 27:56, Mk 15:40 // Mk 16:1

(34) *Many other women from Galilee* [perhaps Veronica]: Luke 8:2–3 // Matthew 27:55–56, Mark 15:40-41, Lk 23:49, 55—24:1, 10–11

(35) Wife? of Cleopas of Emmaus: Luke 24:13–35

(36) Mary, mother of John Mark, at the Upper Room: Mark 14:13–16, Luke 22:10–13 // Acts 1:12–14 // 12:12–13

(37) Church, wife of Christ, symbolic: Revelation 19:1–9 // 22:17

<u>Marys in the New Testament</u>
Mary, mother of Jesus
Mary Magdalene, healed by Jesus, first witness of risen Jesus
Mary of Bethany, sister of Martha and brother of Lazarus
[Wife] of Clopas if this woman is Mary's sister-in-law of John 19:25. See #31 above
The other Mary, mother of Joses and James, called the Less, the Younger, or Son of Alphaeus
Mary, the mother of John Mark in the early church
Mary, a Christian in the church at Rome, Romans 16:6

APPENDIX C: WOMEN IN PAUL'S LIFE

Women in Saul's Life before His Conversion
Acts 8:3: Women whom Paul had imprisoned for following Christ
Acts 23:16–22: Saul/Paul's sister (whose young son later reported to the tribune a conspiracy to ambush both Paul and the soldiers on their way from the barracks to the Temple)

Women Known to Paul through His Missionary Travels

Acts 13:49–52: Fervid Jewish women drove Paul and Barnabas out of Antioch in Pisidia
Acts 16:1–5: Timothy's Jewish mother, married to a Greek, at Lystra
Acts 16:12–13: Women praying on the sabbath by the river in Philippi
Acts 16:14–15, 40: Lydia, hospitable businesswoman aiding Paul and Silas in Philippi
Acts 16:16–18: Fortune-telling slave girl delivered from her master(s) by Paul's prayer
Acts 17:1–4: Leading women of Thessalonica converted by Paul's teaching
Acts 17:33: Damaris, convert after Paul's teaching on Mars Hill, Athens
Acts 18:1–4, 24–28; Romans 16:3–5: Prisca, wife of Aquila, Paul's fellow tentmakers, who taught Apollo more about faith and hosted a church (see also 2 Timothy 4:19)
Acts 21:5–6: Wives who prayed for Paul at the beach in Tyre before he departed
Acts 21:7–9: Four sisters who had gifts of prophecy, daughters of Philip
Acts 24:24–27: Drusilla, Jewish wife of Governor Felix, heard Paul's self-defense
Acts 25:13—26:32: Bernice, sister [and mistress] of King Agrippa II also heard Paul
2 Timothy 1:5: Lois, Timothy's grandmother; Eunice, name of Timothy's mother

Women Co-workers in Paul's Ministry

Romans 16:1: Phoebe, benefactor
Romans 16:6: Mary, hard worker
Romans 16:7: Junia, prominent apostle, converted before Paul, imprisoned with him
Romans 16:12: Tryphene, worker in the Lord
Romans 16:12: Tryphosa, worker in the Lord
Romans 16:12: Persis, beloved hard worker in the Lord
Romans 16:13: Mother of Rufus, a mother figure to Paul
Romans 16:15: Julia
Romans 16:15: Sister of Nereus
Colossians 4:15: Nympha, who hosted a church
2 Timothy 4:21: Claudia's greeting from Paul in prison in Rome to Timothy

Paul's Pastoral Concerns about Women

1 Corinthians 1:11: Chloe reported that loyalties to different men in leadership caused divisions
1 Corinthians 5:1: Stepmother and man in church scandalously living together
1 Corinthians 9:3–5: Wives of Peter and Jesus's brothers who traveled with them
Philippians 4:2–3: Euodia and Syntyche urged to come to agreement with each other
1 Timothy 5:3–15: Paul's instructions about widows in Ephesus church
2 Timothy 3:6–7: Warning about wrong purposes of visitors to "silly" women
Philemon verse 2: Apphia hears Paul deal with Philemon's runaway slave, Onesimus

APPENDIX D: JUDGES: DOWNHILL DEVOTION AND DECENCY

Review this era on pp. 13–14. The judges ruled one or more tribes of Israel but primarily dealt with conflicts with neighboring Canaanite tribes who had been living there before the Israelites arrived. Note two trends in this book: (1) a number of cycles featuring a given judge and (2) the overall downward spiral of decline in morality and unholy religious practice.

First, in the repetitive cycles, the people experienced distress and cried to the LORD for help. In answer to the prayers, a judge would rise up to defeat their enemies. A period of thanksgiving in worship and devotion resulted. Prosperity and peace followed. As the people enjoyed their good times, their loyalty to God wilted in neglect. Their weakness gave opportunity for enemies to step in to harass them. The people would then cry out and the cycle repeated.

Second, trace the story cycles as each one spirals downward with increasingly shoddy worship, decline in social order, and disregard for the covenant with God and its stipulations. The prominent local fertility gods, Baal, the male, and Ashtoreth, the female, appear in stories not only in the era of Judges but also during the Kingdom era. Worship rites included child sacrifice and orgiastic sexual activity with male and female religious prostitutes.

Increasing decadence is obvious in the relationships between men and women in every category: FD = dads and daughters, MS = mothers and sons, BS = brother and sister, HW = married, NM = not married sexual partners, and PP = peers not related by blood or sexual behavior. Don't forget to breathe in the fragrance from the families of Ruth and Hannah.

Chapter	Links between men and women
1	FD, Caleb & Achsah; HW, Othniel & Achsah
2	Description of the spiritual life of Israel and the role of judges
3	Intermarriage with idol worshippers
4–5	HW, Lappidoth & Deborah; PP, Barak & Deborah; PP, Sisera & Deborah; PP, Sisera & Jael
6–7	Gideon defies Baal worshippers, Midianites, and Amalekites, tribal rivalry
8–9	HW, Gideon & wives: NM, Gideon & concubine of Shechem; MS, Shechem concubine & Abimelech; PP, Abimelech & woman on tower
10	More idolatry and judges and repentance, troubles with Ammonites
11–12	NM, Gilead & prostitute; MS, Gilead's prostitute & Jephthah; HW, Gilead & wife; MS, Gilead's wife & sons; ms, Gilead's wife & Jephthah; FD, Jephthah & daughter; BS, Ibzan's 30 sons & 30 daughters; HW, Ibzan's sons & 30 outsider wives
13–16	HW, Manoah & wife; MS, Manoah's wife & Samson; HW, Samson & Timnite wife; FD, father & Samson's Timnite wife; PP, 30 men & Samson's wife; HW, Samson's companion & Samson's wife; FD, Timnite father & Samson's wife; NM, Samson & Gaza prostitute; NM, Samson & Delilah; PP, Philistine rulers & Delilah

17	MS, mother & Micah
18	Blatantly violent, deceptive, false worship for profit
19–20	nm, Levite & concubine/wife? from Bethlehem; FD, Bethlehemite & daughter; PP, old man host & concubine; PP, young servant & concubine; FD, old man host & daughter; NM, Gibeonites & concubine
20	Tribal war of Israelites against Gibeonites and Benjaminites; PP, Israelite warriors & deceased Bethlehem concubine
21	FD, Israelite men & daughters; PP, men & women of Jabesh-gilead; PP, Israelite leaders & 400 virgins of Jabesh-gilead; PP, Israelites & dancers of Shiloh; HW, Benjamites & wives carried off

ENDNOTES

Introduction

1   Adapted from *How to Read the Bible for All Its Worth* by Gordon D. Fee and Douglas Stuart (Zondervan, 1982 and subsequent editions).

1

1   The two emphases I noted in this verse are based upon e-mail correspondence with scholar J. Richard Middleton, Old Testament professor at Northeast Seminary, Rochester, NY. On July 5, 2014, I wrote to him asking, "In Genesis 2:23, does the Hebrew have possessive pronouns for Adam's comment that says Eve is 'bone of my bones and flesh of my flesh' or are the possessive pronouns here inserted for ease of translation?" He wrote back the same day, "In Genesis 2:23 the nouns do have first person singular pronominal suffixes attached (my). ... Often such pronouns are only implied, especially in Hebrew poetry (which tends to omit conjunctions, prepositions, and even possessives."

2   Final lines of "The Agony," poem by George Herbert (1593–1633), from *The Temple* (1633).

3   Luke 24:34.

4   Compare John 2:11 with verses 17–22.

5   Thomas's dark comments in John 11:11–16 and John 14:1–5 preceded renowned revelations of hope.

6   1 Corinthians 15:54–55.

2

1   Exodus 6:20.

2   Genesis 46:34.

3   Acts 2:1–21, especially verses 13 and 15.

4   Attributed to David: Psalm 17:8, 36:7, 57:1, 61:4, 63:7. See also 91:4.

5   From Galatians 4:4.

6   N. T. Wright, prominent New Testament scholar, explains his translation of 1 Timothy 2:11–12 quoted here: "[Women] must study undisturbed in full submission to God. I am not saying that women should teach men or try to dictate to them; rather that they should be left undisturbed." Wright recommends the leisure and space for women to learn with neither gender dominating. *Paul for Everyone: The Pastoral Letters* (London: SPCK, 2003), pp. 21–27.

3

1   Luke 9:23–25, Matthew 16:24–26, Mark 8:34–36; like Matthew 10:33–39; Luke 12:9, 14:26–27, 17:33; like Jesus's service as the Good Shepherd, John 10:17–18.

2   Carolyn Custis James, "Tamar: The Righteous Prostitute," in *Vindicating the Vixens*, ed. Sandra Glahn (Grand Rapids: Kregel, Inc., 2017), p. 45.

3   From 2 Kings 23:25.

4

1   From Job 2:9 and Luke 17:32.

2   The name Job may have come from Jacob and Leah's grandson through Issachar, Genesis 46:13; 1 Chronicles 7:1. See Ch. 3, p. 23. Some translations spell this name "Job" while the NRSV spells it "Jashub."

3   1 Corinthians 1:25.

4   Hebrews 9:4.

5   While these words from Charles Wesley's hymn are appropriate for children's prayers, Dorothy Sayers declared in a speech entitled "Creed or Chaos," delivered at the Biennial Festival of the Church Tutorial Classes Association in Derby, May 4, 1940, that such an image misrepresents Jesus if it implies the slightest indifference to the fatality of sin.

5

1   Genesis 4:1b.

2   John 4:4-42, especially 25–26. See the story of the Samaritan woman at the well in Sychar in ch. 3 above.

3   1 Samuel 16.

4   Leviticus 20:10; Deuteronomy 22:22.

5   From Psalm 51:17.

6   Quotes taken in order from Luke 2:49; John 2:4; Luke 14:26, 18:29–30, and 11:27–28.

7   1 Corinthians 13:7.

6

1   Troy Lacey, "Jacob's Odd 'Breeding Program' of Genesis 30," April 26, 2019, answersingenesis.org.

2   Based on Ecclesiastes 4:12c.

3   1 Kings 11:1–4. The Bible has no stories of polygamy that produced peace and harmony.

4   For Jesus's brothers' disbelief, see John 7:2–5; John brings Mary into his home, John 19:25–27; members of his family in the Upper Room, Acts 1:14; his brothers, especially James, serving in the early church, Acts 12:17, 15:13, 1 Corinthians 9:5, 15:7, and Galatians 1:19.

The Tutorial Reviewed

1   1 Samuel 2:26 and Luke 2:52.

Part III

1. The late Bishop William "Bill" Carl Frey (1930–2020), from his lectures on homiletics at Trinity Episcopal School for Ministry, 1990–96.
2. From Song of Solomon 8:6–7.
3. Book (a.k.a. Song) of Songs. The title means the greatest of songs, similar to "Lord of lords."
4. "Sister, my bride" appears in 4:9, 10, 12, and 5:1, and "my sister, my love" in 5:2. "Brother" appears in 8:1.
5. From 1 John 2:16.

7

1. Ephesians 5:21–33; Revelation 19:5–9, 22:17.
2. For Rebekah's petulance, see Genesis 25:22, 27:46. She never saw Jacob again; the curse sadly did fall upon her (Genesis 27:13).
3. Luke 11:51; Matthew 23:35. Joash murdered the prophet Zechariah, son or grandson of Jehoiada and Jehoshebeath.
4. Luke 8:1–3.
5. Genesis 1:26–28, 2:5-8.
6. From the conclusion of Paul's household instructions on marriage in Ephesians 5:21–33, verse 32.
7. The NRSV avoids "daughters of men" in Genesis 6 verses 2 and 4, though the vast majority of translations read "sons of God" and "daughters of men" in both verses. The meaning of the Hebrew word "Nephilim," translated sometimes as giants, spirit world beings, or fallen beings, remains unclear to scholars.
8. From the Collect for Purity in *The Book of Common Prayer* (New York: Church Publishing, Inc., 1979), p. 355.

8

1. Besides Genesis 1, see also Proverbs 8, especially verses 22–36.
2. Genesis 2:24.
3. Fornication: sexual intercourse between people not married to each other or to anyone else. Adultery: sexual intercourse when one or both parties are married to someone else.
4. 1 John 4:18a.
5. Matthew 7:15–20, 12:33–37, Luke 6:43–45.
6. 2 Samuel 23:39; 1 Chronicles 11:41. Uriah the Hittite was one of the Thirty, David's great warriors.
7. Some early manuscripts omit it, but 1,700 Greek New Testament manuscripts place it either in Luke or John.

Cupid's Confessions

1. "The Celebration and Blessing of a Marriage," *Book of Common Prayer* (New York: Church Publishing, Inc., 1979), p. 423.

2   James 1:5–8.

3   Some examples include Jeremiah 2–3, Ezekiel 16, and Hosea 1–3.

Part IV

1   Based upon 1 Peter 2:4–11.

9

1   From Ecclesiastes 4:12c.

2   From Psalm 111:10.

3   See Matthew 23:14 (omitted in some versions), Mark 12:40, and Luke 20:47. Jesus condemned religious leaders for exploiting widows.

4   Examples of Gentiles exercising great faith in Jesus: a Roman centurion, Matthew 8:5–13, Luke 7:1–10; and a Canaanite/Syrophoenician mother, Matthew 15:21–28, Mark 7:24–30.

5   Respectively, 1 Kings 1:15–21, 28–31; 1 Kings 21:4–7, 15–16; Esther 4:5–17, 5:2–8, 7:2–8, 8:3–8, 9:11–14.

6   Luke 8:1–3.

10

1   Gentiles Jesus healed: this girl; royal official's son, John 4:46–54; Roman centurion's servant, Matthew 8:5–13, Luke 7:1–10.

2   Children healed at fathers' requests: official's son above; epileptic boy, Matthew 17:14–18, Mark 9:14-27, Luke 9:37–42; Jairus's daughter, see p. 106.

3   Matthew 25:45.

4   Jesus's kingdom commends servanthood, John 13:1–35; verse 23 refers to John.

5   Pilate questioned Jesus about his kingdom, John 18:28—19:16.

6   All four Gospels record Peter's denial: see Matthew 26:69–75, Mark 14:66–72, and Luke 22:54–62.

11

1   Deuteronomy 23:1. Isaiah 56:1–8 anticipates Philip's ministry to the Ethiopian Chief of the Treasury.

The Hebrews et al.

1   (1) Apostolic couples traveling together: Peter/Cephas and some of the Twelve, Priscilla, and Aquila; (2) Mary, John, Barnabas, John Mark, Paul, Timothy, and others of the Twelve; (3) Paul, Apollos, and Lydia; 4) Peter, James, Aquilla and Priscilla; (5) Barnabas, Ananias and Sapphira, Lydia; (6) most Christians, especially widows; (7) the Twelve, Barnabas, Mary mother of Jesus, Mary at the Cenacle, and converted Temple priests; (8) Stephen, Philip, the Greek widows, the other deacons, and Silas; (9) Pentecost pilgrims, Paul, Priscilla, and Aquila; (10) Timothy with Greek and Jewish parents; (11) Lydia and the Ethiopian eunuch; and (12) Luke, Titus, and Syntyche.

12

1   Exodus 35:25–29.

A Closer Look at the Hearts of the Matter

1   Acts 6:7.

2   Paraphrased from John 14:2.

3   From Mathew 25:21, 23.

4   Examples: The LORD sent daily manna when the Israelites wandered in the wilderness. Jesus multiplied bread and said, "I am the bread of *life ... the living bread*" (John 6:35, 48, 51). The LORD guided the Israelites in the wilderness by a cloud and a pillar of fire. Jesus said, "I am the good shepherd" (John 10:11, 14). Jesus gave sight to a man born blind and said, "I am the light of the world" (John 8:12). Elijah and Elisha brought life back to two boys near death. So did Jesus and even more, declaring, "I am the resurrection and the *life*" (John 11:25). Finally, the Resurrection verified what Jesus had said, "I am the way, and the truth, and the *life*" (John 14:6) (emphases mine).

Conclusion

1   Ecclesiastes 1:2b, 12:13b–14. The commandments: Exodus 20:1–17, Leviticus 19:18b, and Deuteronomy 6:5.

2   From 1 John 4:20b.

Afterword

1   2 Corinthians 4:7, 11.

Appendices

1   Genesis 3:14–20. A penchant to disobey and distrust God heightens anxiety and strains interaction with the other gender and with God. Both men and women have concomitant concerns about childbirth and food production. In a personal conversation on April 26, 2021, with John H. Walton, Old Testament scholar at Wheaton College specializing in the Genesis accounts, he pointed out that the parallel construction of this passage did not segregate these concerns to one or the other gender but highlighted an aspect of greater concern to women or to men. Women hoped to survive childbirth and to safeguard a young child in the vulnerable early years. Men hoped for physical strength, beneficial weather, and fertile ground to provide sustenance for the family.

2   The risen Jesus commissioned Mary Magdalene to tell the other disciples, "I am ascending to my Father and *your* Father, to my God and *your* God" (emphasis mine). Thomas heard Mary's testimony before his own confession, "My Lord and my God."

3   Joan Comay and Ronald Brownrigg, *Who's Who in the Bible* (New York: Wing Books, 1993), New Testament, pp. 75, 292.

4   William P. Barker, *Everyone in the Bible* (Old Tappan, NJ: Fleming H. Revell Co., 1966), p. 230.